Software Architecture by Example

Using C# and .NET

Paul Michaels

Foreword by Mark Richards

Apress®

Software Architecture by Example: Using C# and .NET

Paul Michaels
Derbyshire, UK

ISBN-13 (pbk): 978-1-4842-7989-2   ISBN-13 (electronic): 978-1-4842-7990-8
https://doi.org/10.1007/978-1-4842-7990-8

Managing Director, Apress Media LLC: Welmoed Spahr
Acquisitions Editor: Smriti Srivastava
Development Editor: Laura Berendson
Coordinating Editor: Shrikant Vishwakarma

Cover designed by eStudioCalamar

Cover image designed by Pexels

Distributed to the book trade worldwide by Springer Science+Business Media LLC, 1 New York Plaza, Suite 4600, New York, NY 10004. Phone 1-800-SPRINGER, fax (201) 348-4505, e-mail orders-ny@springer-sbm. com, or visit www.springeronline.com. Apress Media, LLC is a California LLC and the sole member (owner) is Springer Science + Business Media Finance Inc (SSBM Finance Inc). SSBM Finance Inc is a **Delaware** corporation.

For information on translations, please e-mail booktranslations@springernature.com; for reprint, paperback, or audio rights, please e-mail bookpermissions@springernature.com, or visit http://www.apress.com/ rights-permissions.

Apress titles may be purchased in bulk for academic, corporate, or promotional use. eBook versions and licenses are also available for most titles. For more information, reference our Print and eBook Bulk Sales web page at http://www.apress.com/bulk-sales.

Any source code or other supplementary material referenced by the author in this book is available to readers on GitHub via the book's product page, located at https://link.springer.com/book/10.1007/ 978-1-4842-7989-2.

Printed on acid-free paper

To my wife, Claire, who has always been on, and at, my side,
even when I have not.

And to my dad, who has understood and supported me in everything
that I've done from the minute I was born.

Table of Contents

About the Author xi

About the Technical Reviewer xiii

Acknowledgments xv

Introduction xvii

Foreword xxi

Chapter 1: The Ticket Sales Problem 1

    Background 2

    Requirements 3

        Options 4

        Manual Process 4

        Existing System 6

        Existing System Considerations 7

        Minimum Viable Product 8

    Target Architecture 8

        How to Deal with High Throughput 9

        Widening the Funnel 10

        Multiple Funnels 11

        Message Queues 13

        Message Brokers 14

        Separation of Concerns 16

        Target Architecture Diagram 17

        Proxy 18

        A Note on Cloud Vendors 19

        Why Cloud? 20

Examples.. 21

    External APIs.. 21

    Getting Ticket Availability.. 21

    Ordering a Ticket 25

Summary.. 29

Chapter 2: The Cash Desk Problem **31**

Background... 32

Requirements.. 32

    Options 32

    Manual Process... 33

Target Architecture... 36

    Audit 36

    Event Sourcing 40

    CQRS... 46

    Target Architecture Diagram.. 47

Examples.. 49

    Persisting Events to Memory.. 49

    Persisting Events to Disk 52

Summary.. 61

Chapter 3: The Travel Agent Problem **63**

Background... 64

Requirements.. 65

    Options 66

    Manual Process... 66

    Transactions 67

    Distributed Transactions 71

    Distributed Transaction with Timeout 74

    Book and Cancel... 75

    Hold a Booking 76

Advanced Purchase 76

Business Decision 76

Target Architecture.. 77

Stateful Service 79

Distributed Service 79

Target Architecture Diagram.. 79

Examples.. 80

Project Structure 80

Service Bus Configuration 82

Coordinator 85

Summary.. 90

Chapter 4: The Social Media Problem... **93**

Background.. 94

Requirements... 94

Options 95

Manual Process 96

CQRS.. 97

Target Architecture.. 102

Examples.. 104

Schema Creation 104

Updating the Database 105

Checking the Data 107

Web Service... 107

Accessing MongoDB... 110

The Client 114

Process Data Service 118

Summary.. 122

Chapter 5: The Admin Application Problem 125

Background 126

Requirements 126

Options 127

Manual Process 127

SOLID 129

   Single Responsibility 130

   Open-Closed 133

   Liskov Substitution 136

   Interface Segregation Principle 138

   Dependency Inversion Principle 139

Methods of Extending Software 141

   Hooks 141

   Messages 142

   Injection 145

Target Architecture 148

Examples 149

   Basic Functionality 149

   Extensibility 154

   Custom Functionality 156

Summary 157

Chapter 6: The Travel Rep Problem 159

Background 160

Requirements 160

Options 161

   Manual Process 161

   Caching 162

   Sidecar Pattern 163

   Ambassador Pattern 164

Target Architecture 166

    Containers 167

Examples 168

    Project Structure 169

    TravelRep.CentralApi 170

    TravelRep.App 173

    TravelRep.Ambassador 174

    Containers 182

Summary 196

Appendix A: Technical Appendix **199**

    Chapter 1 199

Index **205**

About the Author

Paul Michaels is the Head of Development at musicMagpie. He started his career as a professional software engineer in 1997. Paul is a regular speaker, published author, and Microsoft MVP. He enjoys programming, playing with new technology, and finding neat solutions to problems. When he's not working, you can find him cycling or walking around the Peak District, playing table tennis, or trying to cook for his wife and two children. You can follow him on Twitter at @paul_michaels or find him on LinkedIn. He also writes a blog at http://pmichaels.net.

About the Technical Reviewer

Kasam Shaikh is an Azure AI enthusiast, published author, global speaker, community MVP, and Microsoft Docs contributor. He has more than 14 years of experience in the IT industry and is a regular speaker at various meetups, online communities, and international conferences on Azure and AI. He is currently working as Senior Cloud Architect for a multinational firm where he leads multiple programs in the Practice for Microsoft Cloud Platform and Low Code. He is also a founder of the community named Dear Azure-Azure INDIA (az-India) and leads the community for learning Microsoft Azure. He owns a YouTube channel and website and shares his experiences over his website (www.kasamshaikh.com).

Acknowledgments

For this book, I have an absolute phone book of people to thank for their help.

Firstly, I have to thank my daughter, Abi, for all the artwork in the book.

Special thanks to Ash Burgess and Kevin Smith for putting up with impromptu requests for a discussion or a review of an idea, and for Kev's painstaking and repeated explanations of event sourcing.

Thanks to Ian Curtis for reviewing my architectural diagram, and to James Little for making me think so hard about architecture that a book seemed a good idea.

The travel industry is very complex, and I don't think I could have landed in a better place, where I had the expertise and advice of both David Hilton and Jagdip Ajimal.

When it came to containers, I found that what I was trying to do kept throwing up roadblocks until Rob Richardson generously offered his time and expertise.

The examples in this book are based on my time working across industries and trying to solve problems. I've been fortunate in my career to work with a number of very clever and talented people. There are probably too many of these to mention, and while they may not have directly helped with this book, I'd like to acknowledge their contribution.

Finally, I'd like to thank the team at Apress – especially Shrikant for dealing with the various twists and turns that the book, and my life, has taken during its creation, and Smriti for bringing me onto Apress in the first place.

Introduction

All the code in this book is available from the following GitHub repo:

`https://github.com/Apress/software-architecture-by-example`

Should you choose to follow along and create the solution for each chapter, it may be helpful to have a clone of the code available for reference.

Note As I'll be working on a Windows machine, what I do will only be tested on Windows; however, again, this is software architecture, not software architecture for Windows, so everything should also work on MacOS, Linux, or any other modern OS: .Net is a cross-platform framework.

Technology

Let's quickly discuss the specific technologies that we're going to choose and why. Firstly, I will use Visual Studio to write all of the code samples in this book. You can download the community edition of this here:

`https://visualstudio.microsoft.com/vs/community/`

You may also wish to use VS Code, which can be found here:

`https://code.visualstudio.com/download`

All of the applications that we create will be in .Net and written in C#. This choice I made simply because it's the language that I'm most familiar with; however, I don't believe there's anything in here that couldn't be translated to any other modern OO development language; after all, architecture should be language agnostic. Most of the principles are broader than a specific language and could apply to any language capable of making HTTP calls.

Setup

In this section, we'll cover the basic setup that you'll need to follow along with the code samples. However, since this is predominantly a book on architecture, you should be able to translate the concepts to any language.

Let's cover a basic setup for those readers that wish to follow along.

Terminal

If you choose to use VS Code, you have a terminal built in; however, there are other options.

Since you're likely to be using Git, you can easily use git bash for the terminal commands; you can download **git for windows** here:

```
https://gitforwindows.org/
```

Another possibility if you're on Windows is the new (at least at the time of writing) Microsoft Terminal. This can be found here:

```
https://aka.ms/terminal
```

Note This is, in fact, an open source product; you can find the source code for it here:

```
https://github.com/Microsoft/Terminal
```

Examples

The title of this book is *Software Architecture by Example*, so it will not surprise you to learn that there are examples in each chapter. The purpose is to propose a problem, suggest one or more solutions, and provide an example of how that solution might work in reality.

What this doesn't mean is that contained within the pages of this book are full, complete, solutions to each problem. To illustrate my point by example, for the first chapter, we address the problem of a business that sells tickets for concerts and festivals.

In that chapter, there are code samples that will compile and run, but those samples are for illustration purposes; there's no website there, but I've made sure that each element of the system is there by proxy – so the website will be simulated by a console app.

How to Use This Book

There are a number of ways that you may choose to use this book. Each chapter has an explanation of an architectural principle, driven by the typical requirement that it satisfies; once this has been explained, there is an example in each chapter.

All of the code for every chapter can be found here:

https://github.com/Apress/software-architecture-by-example

You can choose to follow along and recreate the examples, or you can clone the repo and simply view the code, or you may decide that you're not interested in a specific implementation, in which case, you can simply skip the examples altogether.

Foreword

The topic of software architecture is hard to describe, teach, and learn, mostly because no one really knows what it is. Some say it's the structural aspect of a system, similar to an architectural blueprint of a large office building or skyscraper. Some say it's how different parts of a system interconnect or interact with one another. Others say it's the foundational aspects of a system that meets certain business goals and needs, irrespective of the system functionality. So who's right? Well, in fact, they all are, which is why it's so hard to explain and teach software architecture.

Decades ago, a software architect primarily focused on the technical aspects of a system – how the various parts, or components, of a system interacted with one another through various interfaces, contracts, and protocols. Today, however, software architecture impacts and influences so much more, including business alignment, data, deployment environments, methodologies, platforms, and so on. These intersections and necessary corresponding alignments have significantly expanded the role of a software architect. In addition to technical skills, a software architect must also possess exceptional people skills to be able to collaborate and negotiate with numerous business and technical stakeholders to ensure that the architecture is aligned with all these factors. With all this responsibility in an ever-expanding role, it's no wonder why software architecture is so difficult to understand.

Back in 2010, a well-known architect named Ted Neward came up with the notion of an "architectural kata" – a way of being able to practice software architecture, much in the same way different moves, or forms, are practiced in martial arts. These small, targeted exercises provide a context to practice some of the core skills an architect must hone to become effective – identifying important driving characteristics ("-ilities") that the architecture must support, identifying possible solutions, analyzing the trade-offs of these solutions, and making architecture decisions.

Through the years, I have found that *teaching by example* helps bring students (and readers) from the abstract to the concrete, allowing them to better understand not only what software architecture is but also why it's so vital to the success of any system, which brings me to this book. Through the use of concrete examples, Paul Michaels helps the reader understand some of the core abstract concepts of software architecture. This form of teaching not only makes the connection between the abstract and concrete but also gives the reader a chance to practice these concepts. As Paul states in this book, "In software, as in life, everything has a price." Leveraging practical examples is one way of being able to learn how to perform the trade-off analysis necessary to arrive at the most appropriate architectural solution. After all, as we all know, "...it depends."

—Mark Richards
Founder, DeveloperToArchitect.com
Author of *Fundamentals of Software Architecture* and
Software Architecture: The Hard Parts

CHAPTER 1

The Ticket Sales Problem

When I first started out in IT, the industry was still quite niche. Although many people used computers in their day job, access to the Internet or even a personal computer at home was still a way off for most people. This was around the time that the industry was gearing up to fix the millennium bug: an issue that was prevalent in many systems, because 20 or 30 years earlier, when these systems were written, the programmers had assumed they would have been replaced before the year 2000.

At this time, if you wanted to go and see a band play, you typically had two choices: you physically visited a record shop or ticket sales venue, for which the queues often stretched out of the door, or you used the telephone. These days, you wouldn't have to go far to find someone young enough to not remember such times, but it's worth bearing in mind how far we have come in 20 years!

© Paul Michaels 2022
P. Michaels, *Software Architecture by Example*, https://doi.org/10.1007/978-1-4842-7990-8_1

The queues stretching out of the door of the ticket booths have now been replaced by millions of people accessing a website at the same time to try and buy tickets. In this chapter, we'll be discussing one of the most prevalent issues in the IT industry today: how to cope with massive spikes in traffic.

Background

Our new client, **123 Tickets**, has asked us to replace their existing system. The existing system that they run works fine for most of the year, but the company makes most of their revenue from just three dates, when they are contracted as the main reseller for premier music festivals. Their existing system simply can't cope with the huge spike in sales and frequently crashes just minutes after the tickets go on sale.

The venues are unhappy with **123 Tickets**' ability to cope with the sales, and the contracts are in danger of not being renewed.

Let's have a look at last year's usage. Figure 1-1 shows a graph with the usage and error statistics from last year.

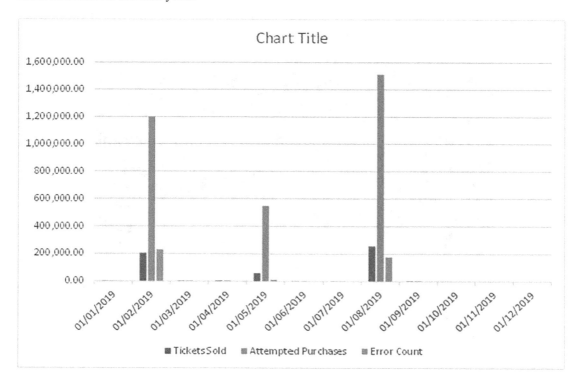

Figure 1-1. *System usage graph*

In Figure 1-1, we can see some very useful information. Firstly, we can see that almost all the business that this company has conducted is during three months of the year; and we can see that when the system is busy, the system errors spike. We can also see that the demand for the tickets far exceeds the supply.

Let's consider exactly what the requirements from *123 Tickets* are.

Requirements

Whenever a system, of any type, is designed, a target should be established. For example, if you're designing a car, your target is a vehicle that transports one or more people between places and is roadworthy (whatever that may mean in your locality). The fact that your car may have three wheels, or two doors, or be painted blue is an optional feature; that is, the car is still a car if it has two, four, or five doors; it's still a car if it is blue or red; however, it is not a car if it has no wheels because it would be unable to fulfill its requirement of transporting people.

When designing a system, it's always worth considering this: what the system needs to do in order to fulfill its basic function. For example, our ticket ordering system presumably needs to allow people to purchase tickets – if it did not, we could not sensibly call it a "ticket ordering system"; but does it need to allow people to purchase ice cream when they arrive at the venue? Probably not, as without that, it's still a "ticket ordering system."

We should, therefore, discuss with the client the list of things that the system needs to do in order to *be* the system; and all the time, we should challenge whether that thing is necessary. To clarify, I'm not saying that anyone should sit in front of a client and argue them into submission about features that they are requesting and willing to pay for; however, we may decide that what is being described is not a single system, but two, or three. Why this is useful is something we'll revisit later in this chapter.

I'm very purposely staying away from any reference to software at this stage, and the reason will become clearer later on.

Let's lay out exactly what we need the system for *123 Tickets* to do. This list is a high-level list of features that the current system provides and which the client has identified we would need to provide:

- Maintain a list of registered users.

- Provide a list of upcoming events for which there are tickets available.

- Allow a user to purchase up to ten tickets for any single event.

- Maintain a count of available tickets.

- Allow users to pick a seat where applicable – not all events are seated (and none of the big festivals are seated).

Now that we've identified what's required, we can discuss the options for providing that.

Options

All too often, software developers and architects reach for the tools that they know best. I'm no exception; any code samples that you'll see in this book are written in .Net. However, exploring other possibilities is not only a useful exercise but also solidifies the requirements in our minds. In each chapter, I'll make the case for solving the problem *without* using technology.

It may seem like a strange thing for a book on software architecture; however, all over the world, people are solving problems without technology; in some cases, that's the best solution. Software design and development costs money; in some cases, it costs a considerable amount of money, and it is not without risk. According to a 2017 report from the Project Management Institute, between 6 and 24% of projects end in failure. These are not only software projects; however, if we accept that as a rough guide, it means that we can reasonably expect around one in ten software projects to fail (source: `www.pmi.org/learning/thought-leadership/pulse/pulse-of-the-profession-2017`).

In our case, *123 Tickets* has an existing system, but let's imagine that our advice to the client is to remove that system and replace it with a manual process. What would that look like?

Manual Process

First of all, we would need to maintain a list of valid users for the system; we could keep this in an address book. Each time someone wished to be added to the system, we would write their name and address into our address book; the maintenance of this book would represent all or part of somebody's job.

Secondly, we would keep a list of events; presumably, we'd use something like a yearly diary to do so; each event would be marked in on the day it was to happen. Somebody would then go through every event for the following two or three months and write on a sheet of paper what, and when, these events were.

Our next step would be to order the tickets from the supplier – when they arrive, our ticket count would simply be that somebody would simply count the remaining tickets for each event.

When a customer phoned up, the operator would go through the following process:

1. Ask for a name, and look them up in the phone book; if they are not already in there, then add them.

2. Check the event that they wished to book a ticket for and ensure that there were sufficient tickets.

3. If the venue is seated, talk through the options for seating with the customer, and establish which tickets would be best.

4. Put the tickets in an envelope (so that they cannot be sold to another person) and take payment details.

5. If the payment fails, or the customer changes their mind before payment is made, the tickets are returned to the pile for that event; otherwise, they are posted to the customer.

In fact, when we consider this, we realize that the manual process is actually quite neat; maybe this is the right approach. Of course, there's a minor snag; even during the smallest festival, over 500,000 attempts were made to purchase tickets; however, before we abandon our manual approach, let's just continue this thought experiment for another few paragraphs.

Let's say that we did need to implement this manually and we had a single operator. What would happen if 500,000 or more people tried to phone in to buy tickets at the same time? Well, the way most basic phone systems work is that the first person would be connected, and until that sale had finished, everyone would get an engaged tone.

So how could we structure this so that, given enough time, we could deal with all these requests? One possible solution may be to divert the calls to an answering machine service (for the purpose of this, we'll assume that the answering machine can take multiple calls at any one time without the caller getting an engaged tone), asking the customer to leave details of the venue and ticket requirements; the operator could then phone each person back as they became free.

Our manual system does have an issue; let's say that our operator is very efficient and can process each call in five minutes; if that were the case, it would take this person around 42,000 hours to process 500,000 tickets. That's around 22 years (based on a 35-hour week)!

How would we solve that? In fact, you're probably thinking that the solution is very obvious: employ more people. If one person would take 22 years, it follows that 2 would take 11. If we had 1000 people, we'd clear the backlog in just over a week. While this may seem obvious, it's easy to forget this knowledge when we start looking at automated solutions.

This is not, however, a new system; the client already has a system in and running, so let's investigate what their existing system looks like.

Existing System

123 Tickets has an existing system. Figure 1-2 shows the architecture for their existing system.

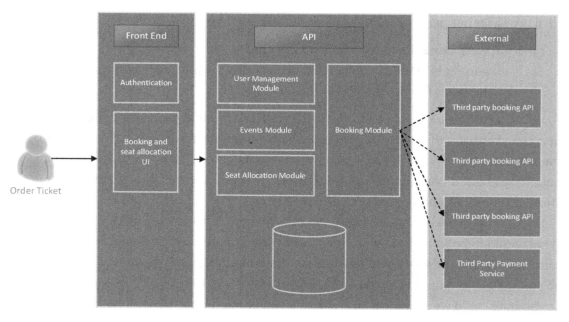

Figure 1-2. *Existing architecture*

There's a lot to like with this current system design; it's modular – that is, each distinct business domain is separated into its own module, and the bulk of the logic is in a separate API. However, let's go back to our manual process and see where we could rethink some of the modules. Our manual process seems to fall naturally into the following four areas:

- Maintain a list of valid users.

- Maintain a list of events.

- Maintain a ticket inventory.

- Ticket ordering process.

While we seem close, the existing system has a module that manages seat allocation, but we've identified that this should probably fit under the ordering process. Further, it appears that we need a ticket inventory; it's very likely that the existing system does maintain a ticket inventory – perhaps it's inside the Booking Module.

Existing System Considerations

When working with an existing system, there's a balance to be struck; often, if a system is already in place and working correctly, this is a much better solution than a system that doesn't exist yet.

Let me clarify what I'm saying here and what I'm not saying. Each system that's in place has a value; that value is comprised of factors, such as the cost of the system to develop, the value that system provides while it's running, the cost of supporting and maintaining the system, and the cost of replacing the system. The latter is a very important figure and is not measured in just pounds and pence.

Replacing a system involves disruption; there's the disruption caused by actually replacing the system, but also, you'll need business domain knowledge, which means you'll be removing people from their day-to-day jobs; the new system is unlikely to look and feel exactly like the old, and so there will be a period when people get used to the new system. There's a risk associated with both creating the new system and implementing it; the risk will vary and can be mitigated, but it will never be zero.

This does not mean that if we have a system that works poorly, we should design around it for fear of breaking anything; however, after we establish a goal, a target architecture, it may influence how, or even whether, we choose to reach that target completely.

Something else that we should come back to at this stage is what constitutes our core system.

Minimum Viable Product

Earlier, we asked what features, about the ticket ordering system, made this a ticket ordering system; in fact, seat allocation may be one feature that is not required in this system. This is the concept of a **Minimum Viable Product**, or **MVP**, and it applies equally to replacing or upgrading a system, as to creating a new one; without defining the scope of the system, you risk any project spiralling out of control, both in terms of cost and complexity.

We should be careful how we go about defining an MVP. Clients and developers are not the only members of the team that are capable of causing *scope creep*. Let's assume that your team has a product manager, and they decide, after speaking to the client, that the system needs an ice cream ordering module; without a documented MVP, it's quite easy for a new user story to get created. In this case, everyone on the project would make an assumption that this functionality did form part of the MVP.

Alternatively, imagine that a system tester finds an issue with the system, along the lines of "The system's ice cream ordering facility is missing or nonfunctional." Again, this may inadvertently result in scope creep.

These are, clearly, contrived examples; and I'm not singling out the roles mentioned – pretty much anyone on, or off, the project could inadvertently instigate scope creep. I'm simply making the point that having determined what our MVP is, we should maintain that document and that everyone in the team should bear it in mind when considering changes, defects, enhancements, or requests.

That said, let's move on to discussing what our target architecture might be.

Target Architecture

A target architecture is just that – something to aim for. You can establish a target architecture, with full knowledge that you're unlikely to ever actually reach that architecture. However, it gives you a guide for how to change your system and where to add new functionality.

Before we get into what our target architecture might look like, we should address the elephant in the room: the inability of our system to deal with the spikes in usage.

When designing a new system, any architectural decisions should be based on the expected usage of the system, plus a sensible margin. For example, in Chapter 5, we'll be discussing an application that is responsible for administering a system; maybe two or three people will be using that at any one time (and that's on a busy day); even if we gave that system 300% leeway for growth, we're still only dealing with under ten users.

I'd like to clarify that if you don't consider performance or concurrency in your system at all, even ten users can overload it. However, in this chapter, we'll discuss techniques for dealing with huge spikes of traffic; here, we have potentially millions of concurrent users – which will be overkill for most systems.

The takeaway here is that in software, as in life, everything has a price: a literal price - i.e., the software costs time (which equates to money) to create and maintain; and a technical price. Ironically, most of the time, the price for dealing with huge spikes in traffic results in a slight hit on speed.

How to Deal with High Throughput

Imagine that we have a funnel and we're trying to pour water into the funnel (Figure 1-3). Instinctively, you'll realize that there is a limit to the rate at which we can pour water into that funnel, above which, the funnel will fill up and eventually, the water will spill out of the top.

Figure 1-3. *Pouring water into a funnel*

If we want to cope with the additional flow, we only have the following choices:

- Widen the funnel

- Use multiple funnels

If we go back to our little thought experiment around how we would do this manually, we see that we have similar choices in our manual system: we can either ask our telephonist to work faster, or we can increase our staff.

Widening the Funnel

Widening the funnel in the case of a web server means essentially one of two things: increase the physical capacity of the server, or increase the capacity of the service.

Server

Increasing the capacity of the server may be very straightforward. If you're hosting this on a cloud provider, you may simply need to press a few buttons, and the server is suddenly a higher specification. If you're hosting this yourself, then you might need to upgrade the physical machine. This approach has some definite advantages: you don't need to change the software – which in turn means that the change is very low risk (in fact, the only risk is that the hardware upgrade may fail for some reason – these days, a very unusual event).

This approach is not to be dismissed. If you have a service that has consistently high traffic, or where spikes are predictable, this can often be a cheap way to keep an existing system working for an extra six months.

However, it does have its downsides. Firstly, you still have a limited capacity; that is, you've widened the funnel, but it's still a funnel, so there is an amount of traffic that will still overload your system. Secondly, you are paying the price for the additional hardware, even if (as in our case) you don't come close to using it for 362 days of the year.

Service

Increasing the capacity of the service can simply (and often) mean optimizing your code. If the service is not processing the required traffic, that may be because you have inefficient code processing the traffic, or it may relate to the speed at which you can insert data into the database.

Most systems that are written equate to a database, with some kind of façade in front of that database to allow the user to insert data into it and to retrieve data from it. What this means is that the bottleneck (or the thin end of the funnel, if you like) is often the database.

Let's spend some time exploring what this might mean and how we could leverage that knowledge to increase our throughput. For the purposes of this illustration, I'll talk about the specific challenges of a relational database; but NoSQL databases have their own challenges; in some respects, they are the exact opposite of those outlined here.

In a relational database, there is always a trade-off between reading data and writing it; databases can write data very quickly, where there are no indexes on the table; however, in this case, it would be almost impossible to read the data, as you would need to execute a full table scan for any query.

As we describe this, a somewhat obvious solution seems to present itself. If you can optimize a database to read but it slows down writes and you can optimize a database for writes but pay the price on reads, what if you could simply separate the two activities?

In fact, this concept has a name: **CQRS**. I first became aware of this after reading a blog post by Martin Fowler; however, he credits Greg Young as the first person to describe it (`https://martinfowler.com/bliki/CQRS.html`).

This does help with throughput; you can, essentially, have an offline process to update your read database from the write; however, you are still writing into a database, which means that you are still limited by the speed at which the inserts can run. Further, you have fractured your system; you now have two data stores to worry about, and the data between them may not be consistent. In some cases, this approach may be an excellent choice; in fact, it may be an excellent choice *in this case*; however, on its own, it will not solve the issue.

Multiple Funnels

If, instead of improving our single funnel, we can increase the funnel count (Figure 1-4), we can potentially accept twice, three times, or twenty times the input data. Of course, we're not proposing to have 20 databases, so what we're really doing is moving the problem. Again, this approach is not free, but before we discuss the cost, let's discuss what this might look like using our funnel example.

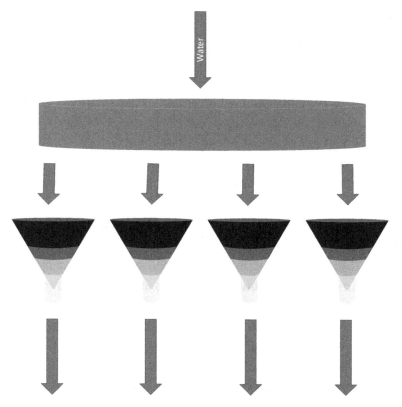

Figure 1-4. *Multiple funnels*

To some extent, the analogy breaks down a little at this point; however, this does serve to illustrate broadly what we're doing. Essentially the trough stores the water as it comes in and releases it at a pace that the funnels can cope with, meaning that each funnel is no longer overloaded as the water comes in.

I think we've taken this analogy as far as it is sensible, so let's think back again to our manual process. We thought that we could increase our throughput by increasing the number of people working through the bookings. We had, in fact, devised a system very similar to this; the answering machine was essentially like the trough above – as calls come in, they are stored on the answering machine. Our telephonists then process the calls at a rate that they can cope with. Here, we have a queue of messages, and that's the approach that we're going to use for our architecture – a message queue.

Message Queues

Let's quickly review exactly what a message queue is, in a way that involves the technology itself – without an answering machine or a funnel in sight.

The principle behind this is simple: a message is sent to the queue, and one or more clients can retrieve and process that message. In practice, there is more to it than that; however, you could (and many people do) implement a message queue as, for example, a table in a database, or a series of files on a disk.

In one of my first jobs, I worked on an EDI (Electronic Data Interchange) system. This system worked in the following way:

1. A sales order would be raised. The system that raised it would add a file to a location on a shared network drive. The file would simply be a comma-separated file in a pre-agreed format.

2. The EDI process would pick up this file (or the oldest file in the directory), read the contents, parse them, and then add the data into a second system (in our case, a CRM system).

At the time, we didn't think of this as a message queue, but that is essentially what it was. With a very small tweak, we could have introduced multiple consumers (by simply moving the file to a second directory before processing).

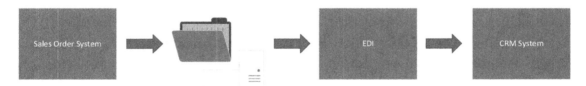

Figure 1-5. *EDI*

The system worked reasonably well; most of the time, the orders came through without issue; however, on occasion, the message (or the file) would either be corrupted in some way or would contain information that we didn't expect. For example, let's imagine that the file looked like this:

```
PROD-CODE-1,3,20.56,2002-02-09
PROD-CODE-2,1,10.00,2002-02-09
PROD-CODE-3,15,0.23,2002-02-10
```

Let's say that this information represents:

Product Code, Order Quantity, Unit Price, Sales Date

Now, let's imagine that we get a file through that looks like this:

```
PROD-CODE-1,,3,20.56,2002-02-09
PROD-CODE-2,,1,10.00,2002-02-09
PROD-CODE-3,,15,0.23,2002-02-10
```

The EDI system is expecting four fields, but seeing five. In this case, the EDI system itself would typically crash, and every subsequent message would start to queue up; even though the subsequent messages may be fine, our system is down.

I imagine you're thinking of several ways that this issue could be alleviated: the file could simply be ignored or skipped if there was an error, or some kind of error handling process could move the file out of the way.

What we needed here was a **message broker**.

Message Brokers

A message broker is a piece of software that is agnostic of the message itself; the message broker has a number of protocols that it can communicate over, but its real value is it acts as an intermediary between the sender and the consumer.

In our EDI case before, the message broker would essentially replace the file system; however, message brokers are pieces of software in their own right. Rather than just communicating via an agreed location on a file share, you communicate via the message broker: send messages to the broker, and take messages from it. In the example before, where the message cannot be read, message brokers provide functionality to move the message out of the way, while others are processed.

Typically, message brokers provide a lot of additional functionality, most of which is beyond the scope of this book. However, since we are talking about using queues, it's worth understanding a little about the infrastructure and setup that may be involved in using a queue.

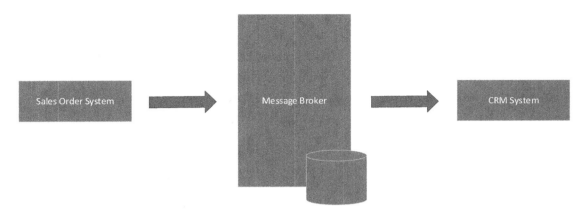

Figure 1-6. *Sales order system using a message broker*

As we said earlier, there's no free lunch here. The message broker provides a great deal of functionality for us; it maintains state, handles failures, takes care of the routing between endpoints (so no one needs to write to a disk share but rather sends a message to an endpoint), and handles transactions; however, as a result, you're no longer simply writing files to a disk on a share, so you sacrifice some performance. In reality, with modern message brokers, using clever caching techniques, the hit is probably negligible (in fact, I imagine if you compared our EDI system back then to any modern message broker, the message broker would be far more performant) – but it's worth bearing in mind that you are introducing processing and complexity into the system.

I'd also like to clarify a point about message brokers; there are dozens of them out there: RabbitMQ, ActiveMQ, ZeroMQ, Apache Kafka, GCP Pub/Sub, Amazon SQS, Microsoft Azure Service Bus, and the list goes on and on. They all have implementation quirks, and they all have advantages and disadvantages. It's probably not even fair to call them all "message brokers"; but my point here is that I'm talking about generics in a world of specifics. I will be covering a specific implementation later in this chapter; but it's very likely that you can pick any message broker and substitute it for the one that we use here.

Now that we've discussed what queues are, and why they can help in this specific scenario, and spoken about such things as message brokers, let's briefly discuss other advantages that using a queue can provide.

Separation of Concerns

The reason that most people choose to use a queue initially is the same as ours: they have a large volume of data, and they want their system to be able to cope with sudden fluctuations in traffic. However, using a message bus provides other benefits. One such benefit is separation of concerns; consider Figure 1-7.

Figure 1-7. *Queue*

Process A can perform some task and put a message onto a bus. **Process B** can read the message from that bus and perform a task. However, Process A has absolutely no dependency or even knowledge that **Process B** exists and vice versa. In fact, we could replace Process A with another process, or several processes, without affecting **Process B** in the slightest.

The second advantage is resilience. Let's imagine that **Process B** fails: if **Process A** were calling **Process B**, then that would cause both processes to fail; however, since all **Process A** is doing is writing to a queue, the messages will simply remain in the queue until such time as they are picked up.

Let's take a real-world and very common use of a queue: email. **Process A** in this case is a website that processes a sales order, and **Process B** sends confirmation emails out to the customer. If the website were to directly call a process to send emails and that failed, then either your entire website would be down or the email confirmations would be lost. However, in the aforementioned situation, the emails are simply left in the queue.

There are many other advantages to using message queues and using a message bus in general (there are messaging patterns other than queues), and I would encourage you to investigate this paradigm further; however, an exhaustive explanation is outside the scope of this book.

Now that we've covered our use of a message bus, let's see our proposed target architecture.

Target Architecture Diagram

Let's move on to a proposed architecture and discuss the advantages and disadvantages.

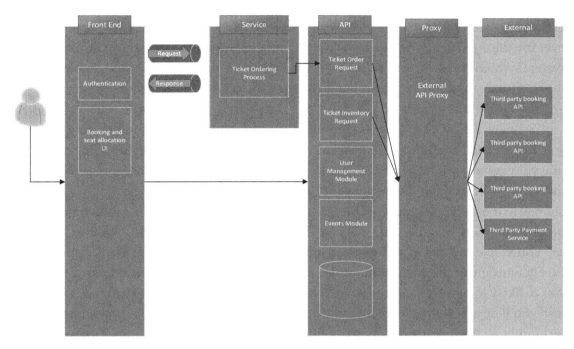

Figure 1-8. *Target architecture*

What we can see in Figure 1-8 is that while the client can access most of the system directly, in order to book a ticket, it enters into a queue. This acts as a buffer between user demand and the capacity of the system. Further, once the ticket request has been added to the queue, we can have one or multiple processes that pick up the request and process it. In our case, this is our new service (entitled "Ticket Ordering Process" in the diagram). If we think back to our manual process, this is our army of staff, listening to answering machine messages one at a time.

You'll notice that there is a second queue going back to the client; this is to allow a response from the process. That is, the service can *reply* to the client to indicate the result of the operation.

Finally, we've introduced a proxy between the rest of the system and the external API. Let's spend a little time discussing why we might wish to do this.

Proxy

The Proxy Pattern was one of the patterns introduced in the Gang of Four book *Design Patterns: Elements of Reusable Object-Oriented Software*. It is very often used in this type of scenario in order to insulate your system against change; since you have no control over the third-party API, you introduce a buffer between your system and external systems which you have no control over. The advantage here is that should the owner of the third-party system decide to change their API, you have only to change your proxy and not your main system.

You may already practice this kind of architectural decision without realizing it; if you've ever used an interface in place of a concrete class, you're probably doing it so that your system can be insulated against change in that class; the change that you're insulating against might be that in your unit test, you mock the class out, but that is a change in the implementation of that class (it's changed from providing functionality to providing no functionality).

I often like to think of real-world examples for such things; in this case, a car is an excellent example of a real-world proxy. Depending on where you live in the world, you're likely to need to undergo some form of test in order to legally drive a car; in that test, you'll be ascertained on your ability to move the car – for example, you'll need to be familiar with what the pedals do and how the steering wheel functions. However, you wouldn't expect any of this to change if you got out of a Ford and into a Volkswagen. Essentially, you've learned to interact with a proxy; the steering wheel may technically function differently in these two makes of car, but the public interface (turn the wheel left or right) remains consistent.

Note   As a quick disclaimer, I'm not a mechanic; the preceding illustration is just that: in fact, I have no idea whether the steering mechanics change between different makes of car; my point is merely that they *could*.

Now that we've explored the theory, let's see what this might look like in a concrete example.

Before we get into the example, let's talk a little about our choice of message broker. I'm going to use a cloud message queue service: Azure Service Bus. The choice of using a cloud service is the real architectural decision here, not the specific vendor; all of the cloud providers have relatively comparable services, and which one you choose will depend on a number of factors – few of which would fall into the category of an architectural choice.

A Note on Cloud Vendors

Certain vendors have variations in services, some of which may better suit your needs; for example, GCP (at the time of writing) doesn't provide a FIFO message bus service – so if that were important, you may be forced to choose another vendor.

My suggestion would be unless you have a very specific need for a particular application, then choose a provider based on the familiarity of the team with that technology. If everyone in your team knows AWS, then pick that.

The caveat here is market availability for people familiar with that technology; a lot of people are familiar with Azure or AWS, and recruiting someone to work with those technologies is relatively easy; however, if you pick some more obscure system, you may find it difficult to find people to work on it. This should not be underestimated; however good a technology may be, you need people to work on it, and you need people to *want* to work on it. If you architect a system that uses a very old or very specific technology, it doesn't matter how good the system design is because either you won't be able to get people to work on it or you'll have to pay a huge premium for them to do so.

I would also advise against an all-in or all-out approach. What I mean by that is that you should try to keep any interaction with your cloud provider abstracted to a sensible level so that if you were to want to move from one provider to another, that would be possible without much work. There are times when this will be difficult, but remember that if your business depends on, say, GCP functions and Google decides tomorrow (or in ten years) that they are moving away from them, you are unlikely to have a say in that decision.

This may sound a lot like I'm heavily advocating the use of containers, and I'm not necessarily. If you have the experience and time to manage a Kubernetes cluster, then maybe that is the right approach, but if you don't, then be very careful about taking on an infrastructure overhead.

Finally, and somewhat at odds with what I've previously stated, it's probably an idea to not distribute your system across too many cloud providers. Although they are all broadly the same, this means that you have multiple places to go and investigate when something goes wrong.

In summary, my advice is to follow the same principles that you would, were the cloud provider a database engine. Good practice is to abstract interaction with the database where feasible in case you needed to change the database engine; but you would be unlikely to interact with both SQL Server and Oracle because the maintenance overhead would outweigh any benefits they might provide.

Obviously, this is an opinion, and it's subject to change; as Kubernetes matures, or other technologies emerge, this may become a solved problem.

Why Cloud?

One of the driving requirements in this case is the ability to cope with a traffic spike. Don't misunderstand what I'm saying here – you absolutely can create a system to handle spikes in traffic that works on-premis.

Note   Just to elaborate on what I mean by "on-premises": by this, I simply mean that you own the infrastructure directly; that is, if the server blew up tomorrow, it would be your responsibility to replace it.

However, what the cloud (any cloud) offers, is a cost benefit. You are not responsible for maintaining the infrastructure, and you only pay for what you use. If you were to build this up locally, you would have to provision a server that could cope with the highest spike in traffic, even though for most of the time, you could probably run the system fine on a far less powerful machine.

If you had multiple jobs that all had different spikes in traffic and you had a massive scale, it might make sense to consider a private cloud; this is the last I'll say in this book about private cloud – while it does have its place, its use cases are very specific; and certainly none of the chapters in this book lend themselves to it.

Now that we've briefly discussed our choices, let's delve into some actual code. We can talk about some other decisions and principles as we go through.

Examples

Clearly, in this book, we won't be writing a full enterprise ticket purchasing system and website. This book is about architectural principles and what they look like in a solid code example; as a result, a large portion of the system will need to be mocked out.

External APIs

The first thing we'll need is something to simulate the third-party systems that we'll be interfacing with. The code for this can be found in the GitHub repo associated with this book:

```
https://github.com/Apress/software-architecture-by-example
```

You can simply clone this repo and run the API; however, if you wish to follow along and create this API yourself, instructions can be found in Appendix A – Chapter 1.

Assuming that you have either cloned the repo or have followed the instructions, then the endpoints for our dummy third-party system will be as follows:

```
https://localhost:5001/externalticketbooking/gettickets
https://localhost:5001/externalticketbooking/reserveticket
https://localhost:5001/externalticketbooking/purchaseticket
```

Now that we've covered the third-party API, let's discuss the two main slices of our system: reading the ticket availability and ordering a ticket.

Getting Ticket Availability

The call to get ticket availability would probably not change between the existing and the new system; however, we have decided to introduce a proxy between our API and the third-party one.

The idea behind an API is to act as a public interface to your system, so if it's designed well (i.e., generically), then you should be able to change the functionality and structure behind the API, without affecting the interface.

Dealing with external APIs   APIs, as you can see from the third-party endpoints before, are about as loosely coupled as you can make one system from another, until such time as you tightly couple them. I like to think of APIs in the same way I think about my mobile phone. I expect my phone to change in the next version, and I half expect it to change so significantly that my current headphones will no longer work with the new phone. If you treat external APIs the same, you'll be in a better place – assume that the API can change and can even change underneath you; be careful about using techniques such as serialization or anything that makes assumptions about the shape of the data that comes back.

If we follow Figure 1-8, we'll see that the interface between the external APIs and our system, in our revised version, is dealt with by a proxy and no longer by the API itself.

Let's drill into a few specific points on retrieving ticket information. In this instance, we will be calling the API directly, rather than via a service. Let's have a look at our implementation for this method in the API.

As you can see from Listing 1-1, this method doesn't call anything directly; it simply calls an in-process proxy.

Listing 1-1. Code – TicketSales.Api/Controllers/TicketInventoryController.cs

```
[HttpGet]
public async Task<IEnumerable<TicketInformation>> GetTickets()
{
    var result = await _ticketService.GetTickets();
    if (result.IsSuccess)
    {
        return result.Data;
    }
    else
    {
        // Log Error
        return null;
    }
}
```

In-process vs. out-of-process proxy   In our example, we're using an in-process proxy here; essentially, we're simply using functionality abstracted by an interface; for example, the API calls an interface method called **GetTickets**. This method then provides functionality to call the third-party API. This type of proxy is often referred to as an SDK. A second type of proxy is where we would, essentially, create another API that we would call, and that API would relay calls to the third party. There's no reason why both of these types of proxy cannot be used in conjunction; however, they provide slightly different benefits. The in-process proxy does abstract the call to the API; however, changing it does mean that you need to (at least) recompile your software – the out-of-process version avoids that. The price that you pay for the out-of-process proxy is the increased complexity of having another API and, essentially, another point of potential failure.

Why haven't we used the queue here as well as in the call to order a ticket? Well, you certainly could do that; however, it does add an overhead to the call. It's also worth considering what benefits that would give. Let's imagine that the system is hugely overloaded, and we call the API to get ticket availability; because the system is so busy, the call times out. Now let's imagine the same scenario, but this time we've added a message to a queue; the call would immediately return, and when the system was successfully able to return the data, it would. However, it's possible that since the call was made, the data that's returned is now out of date.

For the sake of completeness, let's see what the call inside the proxy looks like:

Listing 1-2. Code – TicketSales.ThirdPartyProxy/TicketService.cs

```
public async Task<DataResult<IEnumerable<TicketInformation>>>
GetTickets()
{
    var client = _httpClientFactory.CreateClient();

    HttpResponseMessage response = await client.GetAsync(
        $"{_ticketServiceConfiguration.Endpoint}/GetTickets");
```

```
            if (response.IsSuccessStatusCode)
            {
                string result = await response.Content.ReadAsStringAsync();

                var options = new JsonSerializerOptions()
                {
                    PropertyNamingPolicy = JsonNamingPolicy.CamelCase
                };
                var data = JsonSerializer.Deserialize<IEnumerable
                <TicketInformation>>(result, options);

                return DataResult<IEnumerable<TicketInformation>>.
                Success(data);
            }
            else
            {
                // Log error
                return DataResult<IEnumerable<TicketInformation>>.
                Failure($"Error: {response.ReasonPhrase}");
            }
        }
```

We'll talk more about the proxy and some of the decisions made in this code later. The one thing that I would like to say here is that we are deserializing the JSON data that is returned. I've done this to make the code simpler; however, if you are dealing with an API that you expect to change, then consider manually parsing the JSON. This can be done using a strategy such as XPath – you don't need to rewrite JSON.NET.

While manually parsing the data does represent more work, it should make your system more stable; deserialization is very dependent on the shape of the data being returned. Obviously, if the third-party API was returning a field called **Price** and they change it to a field called **Cost**, there's pretty much nothing you can do – hence the use of a proxy.

Ordering a Ticket

Ordering a ticket is the big change to the system. The previous system was overwhelmed by the quantity of traffic, and so here, we've introduced a buffer (in the form of a queue) between the request and the API. We've already spoken about what a queue is and even how a queue can help with this specific scenario, so let's see what using the queue looks like in practice.

Adding a Message to a Queue

This is the easiest part of the process, especially using something like Azure Service Bus, as there's an SDK that ships with it. In the sample project, the code to actually interface with the Service Bus is segregated into its own project. Listing 1-3 shows what this process looks like.

Listing 1-3. TicketSales.ServiceBusHelper/QueueHelper.cs

```
public async Task<string> AddNewMessage(string messageBody, string
correlationId = "")
{
    var message = new Message(Encoding.UTF8.GetBytes(messageBody))
    {
        CorrelationId = string.IsNullOrWhiteSpace(correlationId) ?
        Guid.NewGuid().ToString() : correlationId,
    };

    await _sendQueueClient.SendAsync(message);

    return message.CorrelationId;
}
```

There's very little to look at in this listing, except the Correlation ID; however, we'll come back to that when we discuss the response message. In fact, we have a second method that sends a message and waits for a reply, shown in Listing 1-4.

Listing 1-4. TicketSales.ServiceBusHelper/QueueHelper.cs

```
public async Task<string> SendMessageAwaitReply(string messageBody)
{
    var correlationId = await AddNewMessage(messageBody);
    var result = await GetMessageByCorrelationId(correlationId);

    return result;
}
```

In the next section, we'll talk about the Correlation ID and discuss how we can use it to get a specific message from the queue.

Getting a Response from the Queue

Typically, using a message queue is one-way communication; the fire-and-forget pattern. However, in our case, we (or rather the person buying the ticket) needs to know whether their purchase was successful. There are a number of ways to deal with this; for example, you could simply send the customer an email, telling them that their purchase was successful.

In fact, this offline processing is the one that you'll see most typically in recent times: either based on the fact that we have your data and so we can guarantee that it will eventually work or based on the fact that the transaction is very likely to work. For example, if I post an update on a chat forum or a social media site, it doesn't really matter if the update doesn't appear for a few seconds, or even a few minutes. Another situation that is similar to ours (with one key difference): if I'm purchasing a product but I'm certain that we will either be able to immediately supply or at least source that product, then we can make the decision to take the order and then process a refund where we can't obtain it.

Our case is a little different: if we can't get the ticket, then we need to let the user know. This could be over email; alternatively, we can use a second queue in order to communicate back to the client. Obviously, we need to match these messages; otherwise, I may be confirming some other person's order.

In fact, if you ever go out to eat in a restaurant, you'll see this exact system in action: the person that takes your order does so on a notepad, which has your table number written on. They hand this to the chef, and at some point in the future, the chef hands back the slip of paper, along with the food order; the serving staff then check that the food matches what's on the paper and return that to the table number that's written on the slip.

In order to achieve the same result, all we need to do is attach our table number to our request; in queue terms, that's typically a **Correlation ID**, although it doesn't have to be. For example, if I have a system-defined piece of information (say, this was a digital food ordering service and I had an actual table number), I can easily use that. The **Correlation ID** is simply a convenience to prevent you having to manually add this to the message each time.

Listing 1-5 shows the code that receives the message and filters for the Correlation ID.

Listing 1-5. TicketSales.ServiceBusHelper/QueueHelper.cs

```
public async Task<string> GetMessageByCorrelationId(string correlationId)
{
    var tcs = new TaskCompletionSource<Message>();
    string returnMessageBody = string.Empty;

    var messageHandlerOptions = new MessageHandlerOptions(Exception
    ReceivedHandler)
    {
        AutoComplete = false
    };

    _responseQueueClient.RegisterMessageHandler(async (message,
    cancellationToken) =>
    {
        if (message.CorrelationId == correlationId)
        {
            returnMessageBody = Encoding.UTF8.GetString(message.Body, 0,
            message.Body.Length);

            await _responseQueueClient.CompleteAsync(message.
            SystemProperties.LockToken);
            tcs.TrySetResult(message);
        }
```

```
    else
    {
        await _responseQueueClient.AbandonAsync(message.
        SystemProperties.LockToken);
    }
}, messageHandlerOptions);

await tcs.Task;
return returnMessageBody;
}
```

I would ask that you don't pay too much attention to the **TaskCompletionSource**, suffice to say that it's a mechanism in .Net to turn an event into an awaitable task. It's only necessary because of a quirk of the .Net Core SDK.

The important aspects of this code start with *AutoComplete = false*. This prevents the message from being immediately acknowledged on receipt. When reading a message from a queue, there are essentially two possibilities: you can read the message and immediately remove it from the queue, or you can read the message and then remove it from the queue at some point in the future when you have determined that you've completed your processing. If we take this back to our restaurant example, *AutoComplete = true* essentially means that service staff would pick up the prepared food from the kitchen, read the table number, and then burn the ticket; if this was not the food that they were expecting, they would be forced to throw it in the bin, as no other serving staff would know where it was supposed to go.

AutoComplete = false has another effect of locking the message; this is to prevent the message from being read, and dealt with, multiple times (our restaurant analogy breaks down here, as more than one person cannot physically pick up the same plate of food).

RegisterMessageHandler then sets up a listener for the events in the system. Once an event is received, we check the **CorrelationId**. If it's the one that we're expecting, then we process it and complete the message (*CompleteAsync*); otherwise, we abandon it (*AbandonAsync* returns the message to the queue).

Summary

Our client's main requirement for this chapter was that we create a system that was able to cope with the spike in traffic that they expect during one of their large ticket sales events.

In this chapter, we established a mechanism for analyzing a system design by comparing the manual process to the proposed automated one. We will conduct the same exercise for all subsequent chapters. If you follow this process and decide that, in fact, a manual process is faster, cheaper, safer, or simpler, then you should think very carefully about whether an automated system is the best approach.

We've investigated the principles behind a message broker, along with other strategies for coping with spikes in traffic. After discussing the value that an existing system holds, we analyzed ways to quantify that value, along with establishing a requirement for a minimum viable product.

By leveraging a cloud message broker offering, we've managed to not only alleviate the issues with the spikes in traffic but also ensure that for most of the year, we're not paying for infrastructure that we simply don't need.

We've covered some of the peripheral benefits of using a message broker for intersystem communication and the benefits and caveats behind using a cloud provider, along with some considerations when choosing one.

Finally, we've spoken about how you can insulate your system design against external (and internal) change to make the system more maintainable and extensible.

CHAPTER 2

The Cash Desk Problem

Cash is becoming an outdated concept. Many people pay, even small amounts, by card or even using their phones. Companies are not missing the decline in cash sales on the whole; cash is a security risk – it can be stolen by people both outside and inside your organization; cash can be forged; and, however stringent your checks, eventually, you will find that you've accepted at least some forgeries. That said, cash is still widely used, and so it must be managed and accounted for.

If your customer pays for their bill using a credit or debit card, or even a check, the transaction is recorded automatically; however, at the end of a shift, it's not inconceivable that a cash desk would be off balance by a small percentage. At a busy shop or restaurant, £20 notes can easily be mistaken for tens; people borrow change from tills without properly accounting for it, and so on, and so forth.

In this chapter, we'll discuss some approaches for solving this, seemingly simple, problem.

© Paul Michaels 2022
P. Michaels, *Software Architecture by Example*, https://doi.org/10.1007/978-1-4842-7990-8_2

Background

EZ Bolts are a large DIY chain. They have approached us to design a new cash desk system for them. They currently have 200 outlets across the world, typically small shops selling basic DIY products: from manual tools (such as hammers and screwdrivers) to larger equipment (such as angle grinders, jigsaws, and drills).

The chain has bought several smaller chains and individual shops over the last few years, and they are all operating different systems, so the main requirement is to consolidate everything into a single system. Around 80% of their sales are still cash.

Having spoken to the managing director, he complains that his biggest issue is that either some sales are not being entered into the existing checkout systems or they are being entered incorrectly; however, the existing systems (which are largely manual) don't give any indication of what might be happening.

Requirements

As with the previous chapter, we should first consider what we must have as an absolute minimum in order to fulfill our requirements. In this case, the requirements are new. Having discussed these with the client, we've established the following as a minimum viable product (MVP):

- Records cash transactions across all the stores.

- Ability to view the balance of an individual till.

- Be able to see the current cash balance across the entire estate.

- An audit of the transactions.

Let's think about how we could provide this functionality to the client.

Options

Although the requirements here are relatively straightforward on the face of it, we are dealing with financial transactions here, and this means that we are restricted in some respects to what we can do; for example, let's imagine that our cash desk system is backed by the following table:

CashDeskId	Balance
001	254.76
002	1,239.45
003	68.91

Now, let's imagine that a customer comes back into one of the shops and wishes to return something. You have a look at the product; in this case, let's say it's a hammer: the price tag says £25.50; however, the customer claims that they paid £30.00 for it last week. They came to cash desk *001*, so how can you tell what you charged the customer?

As before, let's consider the manual option, and hopefully the solution will present itself.

Manual Process

The manual process for this is very well documented: bookkeeping predates computers by thousands of years.

Note   Given that this is a cash desk system, we'll talk about using the single-entry bookkeeping system. An explanation of accounting systems, or a comparison between this and a double-entry system, is way beyond the scope of this book.

For our manual system, we can imagine that the entire system would essentially be recorded on a piece of paper. When someone enters the shop and makes a purchase, the shopkeeper accepts the money and then writes down what has just been sold, for example:

01-10-2020	Hammer	£30.00

At the end of the day, or the end of the week, the shopkeeper might scan down the page and add these figures up; let's see what that might look like:

01-10-2020	1 × Hammer	£30.00
01-10-2020	1 × Philips Screwdriver (PH3)	£15.35
01-10-2020	1 × Socket Set (14pc ¼ in)	£20.02
02-10-2020	2 × Hinge (Zinc Plated Steel – 75×49×1.4)	£1.54
03-10-2020	2 × Nails (70×2.65 – 500g Bag)	£6.10
03-10-2020	Total	£73.01

We haven't exactly made a fortune, but this is the basics of single-entry bookkeeping: you simply write down what you sold, or bought, when the transaction happened, and how much it was for.

Note   It's worth pointing out here that while we have been asked to create a cash desk system, we have not been asked to create an accounting system. Our task is to record what is in the cash desk only.

Before we look at the other requirements, let's for a second imagine that, in our shop, one of the staff is dishonest. Ultimately, if you are employing someone that is dishonest, there are limited things that you can do to protect against that; but let's for a minute see the kinds of things that they may do:

- They may accept money for an item but not write down the transaction and never put the money in the till.

- They may alter existing records such that it appears that less money has been taken than expected and keep the difference themselves.

- They may add credits that weren't made – again, keeping the difference themselves.

Some of these threats would be mitigated by a combination of a stock take and having the member of staff put their name against the records that are entered; obviously, a dishonest person may decide that adding their real name to such record was not in their best interest.

I'm not trying to suggest that dishonesty is rife among people who work in DIY stores, or indeed especially in any industry; but if you lock the doors to your car and house, then you presumably also consider it prudent to guard against dishonesty if it's practical to do so. Let's keep this in mind as we investigate other facets of the system.

We have another requirement here, though; that is that we need to see the cash balance across all of the stores. In order to achieve this, we could instigate some form of central ledger. Let's play this scenario through:

1. The customer enters a store in Basingstoke and buys a hammer; he pays £30.00 and takes it away.

2. The shopkeeper records the transaction as before but also phones up the head office in Manchester and tells them about the transaction.

3. In the head office, the person on the end of the phone records the transaction on another slip of paper like this:

01-10-2020	Basingstoke	1 × Hammer	£30.00

This looks like it would work, but what about the case where the records get out of sync? Let's imagine that the phone line to Manchester is engaged, or another shop accidentally gets recorded as Basingstoke.

What we would need here is a single source of truth; so perhaps the cashier, instead of writing the transaction down himself in a ledger, simply writes down the product, amount, and date on a Post-it note. Then, periodically, someone phones that through to the head office. Now, we don't have a ledger locally, so when we want a balance, we would phone up Manchester and ask them to produce one.

This process does sound a little bizarre – which is a nice indication that an automated system may be needed (or that it's the wrong system).

In fact, if we are to store the information in multiple locations, then we effectively have two choices: either, as above, we essentially ship the information to the "main" store, or we operate some form of reconciliation. Let's imagine what the reconciliation might look like.

The shopkeeper records the sales and, as before, phones them through to the head office; but now, at the end of the day, he phones the head office and, one by one, goes through the transactions that he's recorded; where a conflict occurs, a decision must be made each time as to which records are correct.

Again, let's bear this in mind as we discuss how we could deal with this using an automated system; but before we do, let's just make one point: unlike in Chapter 1, where the manual process was completely unworkable due to volume, the manual solution here is **not** unworkable at all. Admittedly, it would be time-consuming, prone to error, and potentially leave the business open to a small amount of fraud, but it definitely *could* be done.

As an architect, if you have been paid to design such a system, it is incumbent on you to point out the quickest and cheapest possible way to implement such a system, and in this case, that is a manual system. The drawbacks of the manual system are also (roughly) quantifiable; for example, the manual system is more time-consuming; let's do a quick check of how many additional man-hours we're talking about – the time to write down the transaction, the time to phone the transaction through, the time of the person at the head office, etc. Once we have some figures for this, we can convert that into a cost; that is the cost of not implementing the system, and it may be far lower than the cost of implementing the system.

Further, the manual system doesn't have to be that manual; a shared Excel spreadsheet or Google Docs may solve some of the issues that a manual system creates.

For the purpose of this chapter, we'll continue under the premise that a manual system was not acceptable for reasons already outlined.

Target Architecture

So far in this chapter, we've established some clear goals: we need a system that can record cash transactions in all stores, provides an ability to view those transactions, audits those transactions, and is able to provide a cash balance across the estate, or for a single store.

In the previous section, we've discussed how storing the information in a coarse way, such as the balance for each store or till, would be unworkable, as it doesn't provide sufficient audit capabilities; so let's now discuss how we could provide audit capabilities.

Audit

For the purpose of illustration, we'll discuss how this may look in a sales order document that is placed using a web application. I'll explain why I've diverted to this example later on and relate it back to our specific case study.

There are essentially two ways that you can audit any system, and they relate to the way that you would audit such things in real life: if you receive an order and you keep the order document, that serves as its own audit; the second option is that you record separately after you've received the order. Looking at these options, the concept of keeping the original document seems, intuitively, to be the better option because you are able to refer back to what the customer saw and you retain the original context. You also reduce the risk of mistakes during the act of recording the transaction.

The principle is true for computer systems too. When an order is placed, it is frequently sent from the client to the server as a JSON or an XML document (recently, XML has fallen out of favor, so for the purpose of simplicity, we'll focus on JSON).

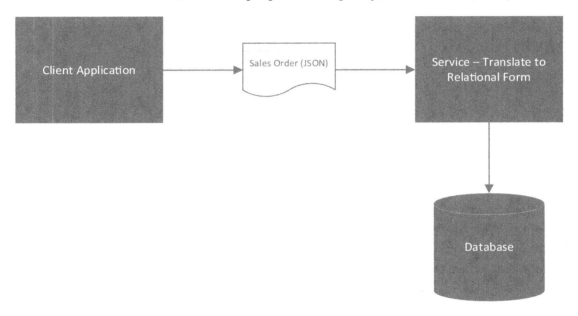

Figure 2-1. *Typical audit*

As is shown in Figure 2-1, most systems take the approach that when an order (or any document) is received, they convert that data into a relational structure and store it in the database. This works well most of the time; however, we should accept that this approach is almost guaranteed to lose data; at the very least, it is changed from that which was entered by the customer. Let's see how.

Imagine that the customer has seen a screen such as that shown in Figure 2-2.

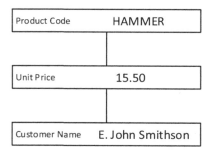

Figure 2-2. *User sales order view*

The user has placed this order, and the fields on the screen have been converted into the JSON document.

Listing 2-1. JSON Representation of Sales Order

```
{

        "ProductCode": "HAMMER",
        "UnitPrice": "15.50",
        "CustomerName": "E. John Smithson"
}
```

In Listing 2-1, we can see that the contents of the screen have been correctly and faithfully represented in the message to the service. Now, let's consider what the relational database may look like that stores this information (we'll use SQL Server):

Field Name	Type
ProductCode	VARCHAR(30)
UnitPrice	DECIMAL
CustomerFirstName	VARCHAR(30)
CustomerLastName	VARCHAR(30)

This doesn't look like an unreasonable table design; perhaps the customer fields would be separated into their own table, but they remain here for the purpose of the point that I'm laboring (and which I'm sure that you've already guessed): who has placed this order?

The customer name that was entered does not fit neatly into the fields that we have available. You might suggest that we store "E. John" as a first name, and perhaps that would be sufficient in this case; but you have *changed* the data, and you have lost its *context*. In fact, we have *designed* a system to lose data. I could further labor the point by listing examples where certain cultures give their last name before their first name, or where surnames are hyphenated, or people that have two last names.

If this is our audit, then can we comfortably say to the customer that the price of the hammer was 15.5, but we have changed some of the fields. The limit for the **ProductCode** field is 30 characters, so what if (through bad system design) we returned a product code that was longer than that?

Let's continue with the acceptance that storing the original document would be good in this situation because it's closer to what the customer has seen on their screen. However, in our system, the customer will never see this information; only the staff will see that information. Well, the reason I started with a sales order that the customer can see is to illustrate that we are altering the information.

Let's return to our reconciliation that we discussed earlier. Money has changed hands, and we need an accurate record of what happened at the time. Let's imagine that in our example before, the routine that parsed the data from a JSON document to create the record in the table has a bug: somehow, instead of entering **15.5** into the cost, **£15.5** was entered instead (and the user interface allowed it). In this instance, one of three things is likely to happen:

1. The system fails silently, and there is no record of the transaction whatsoever – **this is by far the worse outcome**.

2. The system fails, but only the cost is omitted.

3. The system crashes, and the cashier must deal with the problem while the customer waits – as bad an outcome as this is, it is preferable to the alternatives.

Now, imagine that instead of trying to parse the data, we just accept it, exactly as it was entered. The customer can now leave the shop, and we've recorded the transaction. We may not be able to parse it or add it up, but we have the document, so no data is lost, and the customer is unaware of an issue.

Further, if we accept the entire document and store that information, then why should we not use this, unadulterated information, as the source information for the entire system.

Event Sourcing

Event sourcing is the idea that the current state of a system is simply the cumulation of all the things that have happened to that system since its inception. An excellent example of an event-sourced system that you are likely familiar with is a chess board.[1]

Figure 2-3. *Chess board (credit: John Pablok)*

Figure 2-3 shows[2] the initial state of a chess board; now let's consider a chess board that has changed since this point.

---

[1] The earliest reference I can find to event sourcing as a defined architectural pattern was by Martin Fowler from 2005 (https://martinfowler.com/eaaDev/EventSourcing.html). Greg Young has also written and spoken extensively about the subject.

[2] https://opengameart.org/content/chess-pieces-and-board-squares

Figure 2-4. *Chess board state changed*

Figure 2-4 shows the same board in an altered state. For anyone that is unfamiliar with the rules of chess, there are in fact many ways that the board could have changed from Figure 2-3 to Figure 2-4. When you play a game of chess, the game is recorded in the following fashion:

1. d2 d4

2. d7 d5

Note   The chess board is given coordinates, starting with A1 at the bottom left-hand corner and running to H8 in the top right – the coordinates are that of the pieces on the board. Unless you're interested in learning about chess, this is probably as much information as you'll need to know (and if you are, then that falls well beyond the scope of this particular book).

The point here is that there is more than one way that the board could have moved from its initial state to the current state; however, by recording the *events* that occurred, we can recreate the state; but more: we can recreate the state at any point during the game. This is the principle behind **event sourcing**: you record everything that happens to the system and thereby are able to recreate the system **from those events**.

41

The same is true for our cash desk system. Let's imagine the following set of transactions:

1. Deposit 100.00 to till 001

2. Sold Product Code "HAMMER" for 15.50 from till 001

3. Deposit 100.00 to till 002

4. Sold Product Code "PHSCREW13" for 14.21 from till 001

5. Sold Product Code "HAMMER" for 15.50 from till 002

The balance of till 001 should be 129.71. The current *state* of the system depends on the events that created it; however, depending on your requirements, that *state* can appear in any way which makes sense. This means that we can have a view on till 001, a view on till 002, or a view across all tills.

Immutable Events

It's important to realize that these events are (and must be) immutable, partly because changing events in this specific system would constitute fraud, but also because you can't use events as a source if they are likely to change. Let's consider the consequences, were we able to change an event. Taking the events from the previous section, let's alter line 3:

1. Deposit 100.00 to till 001

2. Sold Product Code "HAMMER" for 15.50 from till 001

3. Deposit 90.00 to till 002

4. Sold Product Code "PHSCREW13" for 14.21 from till 001

5. Sold Product Code "HAMMER" for 15.50 from till 002

The balance for till 002 should be £84.50, but now the system believes that it's £74.50. Technically, this means that any existing systems that are currently built would now be at odds with the data; if you rebuilt the state, the data would change.

Note   In financial systems such as this, changing past events, even if it were technically possible, leaves a trail of breadcrumbs back to the invalid entry. The £100 deposit didn't come from thin air and so that deposit will be recorded in multiple places and possibly multiple systems.

Having said that, imagine that you have made a mistake – instead of typing 15.50 for the hammer, you typed 115.50 by mistake.

How to Change Immutable Events

In fact, there are two ways; however, they both follow the principle that you add a new event to correct the old event. The first solution is to add a new one to *correct* the last one. Let's take the case of our mistaken sales figure of the hammer:

1. Deposit 100.00 to till 001

2. Sold Product Code "HAMMER" for 15.50 from till 001

3. Deposit 90.00 to till 002

4. Sold Product Code "PHSCREW13" for 14.21 from till 001

5. Sold Product Code "HAMMER" for 115.50 from till 002

The way to correct this is to simply add another event:

1. Deposit 100.00 to till 001

2. Sold Product Code "HAMMER" for 15.50 from till 001

3. Deposit 90.00 to till 002

4. Sold Product Code "PHSCREW13" for 14.21 from till 001

5. Sold Product Code "HAMMER" for 115.50 from till 002

6. Adjustment for -100.00 on till 002

Generally, this is not considered best practice, simply because it's more complex and therefore less obvious what has occurred. Further, if we were using a double-entry bookkeeping system, unpicking the transaction would be extremely complicated.

Note   In a double-entry system, the transaction is recorded against multiple accounts; for example, in the UK (at least at the time of writing), 20% of the transaction would have gone to a VAT account. Reducing this amount by the amount of VAT that would have been included in the additional 100 would, at the very least, be complicated but, more importantly, would leave the books in an unclear state.

The second, and by far the preferred option, is to undo the entire transaction by negating it, meaning that we would, in fact, add two transactions, for example:

1. Deposit 100.00 to till 001

2. Sold Product Code "HAMMER" for 15.50 from till 001

3. Deposit 90.00 to till 002

4. Sold Product Code "PHSCREW13" for 14.21 from till 001

5. Sold Product Code "HAMMER" for 115.50 from till 002

6. Refund Product Code "HAMMER" for -115.50 from till 002

7. Sold Product Code "HAMMER" for 15.50 from till 002

This is much clearer, as we can now see exactly what happened and why.

In our case, after several years of running this cash desk system, we may find that the volume of data becomes very large. In this case, reading every event from the beginning of time may no longer be practical; we shall discuss the concepts of **projections** and **snapshots** next and how that can help alleviate this issue.

Projections and Snapshots

The concept behind a projection is simply that we represent the event data in a particular way. The key, and pretty much only, rule here is that we cannot change the underlying events. What this means is that we can build a projection based on our cash desk, which represents the balance of a till. We could take a snapshot of this at the start of each day: a sort of running total. We can then apply the events after that snapshot was taken to get an up-to-date picture.

Let's consider what a real-life projection may look like:

1. 2021-05-01: Deposit 100.00 to till 001

2. 2021-05-01: Sold Product Code "HAMMER" for 15.50 from till 001

3. 2021-05-01: Deposit 90.00 to till 002

4. 2021-05-01: Sold Product Code "PHSCREW13" for 14.21 from till 001

5. 2021-05-01: Sold Product Code "HAMMER" for 115.50 from till 002

6. 2021-05-01: Refund Product Code "HAMMER" for -115.50 from till 002

7. 2021-05-01: Sold Product Code "HAMMER" for 15.50 from till 002

8. 2021-05-01: Total for till 001 – 129.71

9. 2021-05-01: Total for till 002 – 105.50

As you can see, the history looks the same as we saw before, but items 8 and 9 represent totals for that day.

So the difference between the two concepts is that a projection is a particular view of the events that we have; for example, maybe we want to see a projection of the number of hammers sold – the data doesn't change; we just see a particular view of it. A snapshot is essentially a version of that projection at a given point in time.

The reason for using a snapshot in event sourcing is exactly the same reason that you would use the same method in real life: each day, it would be time-consuming to add up every transaction for every previous day. In our particular case, we would probably be fine for a very long time – we're storing very simple data, and adding numbers up is what computers do very well; however, at some stage, it would start to have an impact on performance.

The beauty here is that you can add projections to the data as and when you see fit. Because we have the underlying events, all we're really doing is creating a summary representation of those events; we could create a projection per till per day initially, but then we may decide in six months that we wish to create a projection against all the tills for each day, or all the tills for each month. We could create a projection that allowed us to see what the balance of the tills were at 12 p.m. each day; clearly trying to do that if you only stored the current balance of each till would be impossible!

Aggregates

Our system won't use aggregates, or it will only use a single aggregate (cash desk), but it's worth just adding a note as to what these are and why we should bear this in mind for more complex systems.

Essentially, an aggregate represents a single, whole area of data (you might think of this as a business entity). In our case, that is the cash desk, and so it's all a single aggregate; but we could, for example, imagine a situation where we had a stock system; deliveries of stock coming into the warehouse would represent a separate aggregate. Effectively, this forms an independent event stream.

There are a few reasons for doing this; although projections can encompass multiple aggregates, they are likely to be confined to just one; for example, the data that we need to know about the cash desk is unlikely to include stock levels. This means that we can read the relevant stream faster. Aggregates also give us a way to organize our code – the logic to determine the current state of a given aggregate can live in a single place, which maps to its general area of functionality.

Aggregates exist as a concept outside of event sourcing, but for the purpose of this chapter, that's all we'll be saying on aggregates.

We now have a system where we can store events and calculate state from those events. There is just one small issue with this approach, and that is that we can no longer read and write from the same channel.

CQRS

When you have a standard data store, you can easily read and write from, essentially, the same channel; that is, if I have a **SALES** table, I can add to the table, read from the table, and even update the table; in most cases, the RDBMS will just handle this process for me; it does this by using various locking techniques, for example:

```
SELECT * FROM SALES

'DRILL', 42.30, 1
'PHSCREW13', 14.21, 1

INSERT INTO SALES (ProductCode, Amount, Quantity)
VALUES ('HAMMER', 15.50, 1)
```

```
SELECT * FROM SALES

'DRILL', 42.30, 1
'PHSCREW13', 14.21, 1
'HAMMER', 15.50, 1
```

Note   Although I've used a SQL syntax here, the principle applies across any managed data store.

Now, let's imagine that we're using an event-sourced system; there will be a process in between the point that the data is inserted and the data being available to retrieve. The result of this is that we simply cannot use the same process for reading as for writing.

As luck would have it, using a different "channel" for reading and writing is, in fact, a well-known paradigm in system architecture. Typically, it's implemented intentionally as a strategy to take load away from the database. In our scenario, we're just going to end up with it as a consequence of making our system event sourced.

Target Architecture Diagram

Now that we've now been through the basic tenets of the system, let's have a look at the target architecture diagram.

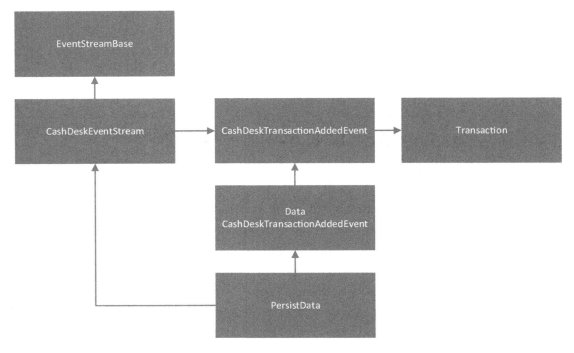

Figure 2-5. *Target architecture*

Figure 2-5 shows the target architecture. In the example section, we'll delve into the code in some depth, but for now, let's consider the general flow.

Each time some*thing* happens to the system, that *thing* is termed an event; in our case, we have a single event, and that is that a cash desk transaction has been added to the system (***CashDeskTransactionAddedEvent***). That event contains details of the transaction itself (*Transaction*) – that is, the amount, the date, the product description, etc. Next, there is a class that holds and manages the stream of events; that is, each time an event occurs, something adds that event to a collection of events – that's the ***CashDeskEventStream***; this contains a list of things that have happened to the system, along with logic relating to what to do with an event when it occurs.

As the events are added, any projections will be built up, and that is where we will read data from – not from the events.

Now that we've seen the principle behind event sourcing and CRQS, let's see an event sourced system in action.

Examples

Before we get into examples, it's worth bearing in mind exactly what event sourcing is and what it is not; it's a philosophy; it is not a framework, or a package, or a toolset. There are tools that are built for the purpose of making event sourcing easier; some of the well-known ones are:

Event Store DB (`www.eventstore.com/`)

SQL Stream Store (`https://github.com/SQLStreamStore`)

Marten DB (`https://martendb.io/`)

In our example, we're not going to use one of the event-sourcing tools or frameworks available. I've chosen to start from scratch mainly because the systems currently available have setup requirements that would simply clutter the example and because configuring this manually is not that complex. Mostly, I feel we can demonstrate the principle better by creating an example from scratch.

Note   I'd like to add a caveat here: the example that we're going to create is a minimal example for the purpose of demonstration; it is not (and is not intended to be) a framework in and of itself.

As with all the examples, you can find the complete code on GitHub here:

`https://github.com/Apress/software-architecture-by-example`

Persisting Events to Memory

For any system, once you've started thinking about the design, it's easy to get carried away with the details and miss the focus of the system. Essentially, what we are doing here is storing changes of state; as a result, our primary focus should be on the class that does that; in our case, that's the **CashDeskEventStream** class. The purpose of that class is simply to manage the addition of an event to the *aggregate* (i.e., to the cash desk stream). In our case, we have very minimal logic here, which is to maintain a running total of the balance of each cash desk in the system.

We're going to split this class into two parts so that we have a generic base for any other aggregate classes that we may create; let's see the base first.

Listing 2-2. Code – CashDesk.Server/EventStreamBase.cs[1]

```
public abstract class EventStreamBase
{
    public string StreamName { get; set; }
    public List<object> Changes = new List<object>();

    public void Apply(object theEvent)
    {
        When(theEvent);
 Changes.Add(theEvent);
    }

    protected abstract void When(object theEvent);
}
```

Each[3] stream needs a list of changes to that stream, some way to reference it (i.e., a name), and a method that allows a change to be applied; hence, we have a ***StreamName*** property to store the name, a *Changes* property[4] to store the events, and a method to apply a new change (***Apply***).

This simply defines a structure for our actual class, which looks like this.

Listing 2-3. Code – CashDesk.Server/CashDeskEventStream.cs

```
public class CashDeskEventStream : EventStreamBase
{
    public Dictionary<string, decimal> CashDeskBalance { get; set; } =
            new Dictionary<string, decimal>();

    public void AddTransaction(CashDeskTransaction transaction)
    {
```

---

[3] Alexey's Place: https://zimarev.com/blog/event-sourcing/entities-as-streams/ (April 22, 2020)

[4] The **Changes** collection is *public* here so that you can see what's in it while you create the system. This should be *protected* so that it cannot be directly accessed outside of this class and its children.

```
    var trans = new CashDeskTransactionAddedEvent()
    {
        Transaction = transaction,
        IsNew = true
    };
    Apply(trans);
}

protected override void When(object theEvent)
{
    switch (theEvent)
    {
        case CashDeskTransactionAddedEvent transactionEvent:
            var transaction = (CashDeskTransaction)transactionEvent.
            Transaction;

            if (!CashDeskBalance.ContainsKey(transaction.CashDeskId))
                CashDeskBalance[transaction.CashDeskId] = 0;

            CashDeskBalance[transaction.CashDeskId] +=
            transaction.Amount;
            break;
    }
}
}
```

Let's break this apart and analyze the constituent parts. **AddTransaction** is probably the easiest to start with, as it essentially does nothing; we accept a transaction and translate that to an event. The event is then passed back to the base class and subsequently back up into the concrete class for domain-specific logic to be applied (then handled by the **When** method).

Note   The **IsNew** flag is used to determine whether an event has occurred since the data has been read from the stream; this means that we only persist back the changes since the last time the data was read.

The **When** method handles the logic relating to an event being added to a stream; in this example, that simply involves keeping a total of the cash desk.

The next stage is to take the stream that we have in memory, and write that out to the disk.

Persisting Events to Disk

Before we get into the specifics of how we are doing this, I'll reiterate that this example is for illustration purposes. In our particular example, I'm going to persist the event stream to disk. The stream will be stored in a set of files, containing the stream name, along with a date and time stamp. Each file will contain only the differences since the last file was written, for example:

```
2021-01-01-10-41-07-Stream1
2021-01-01-10-56-07-Stream1
2021-01-01-10-57-08-Stream1
```

Each file will contain JSON that lists the changes since the last file was written.

Let's divert for a second and discuss why I've chosen to do this and why you probably shouldn't in any production environment.

During the research for this book, I came across a number of articles and examples of event sourcing, but most of them glossed over exactly how the data is written (persisted); I didn't want to do this, but I also didn't want to have a section describing the setup of an MS SQL database, or CouchDB, MongoDB, or one of the other NoSQL offerings for that matter.

Given that, I thought about what the database is actually doing for us, and the answer (at least as far as an illustration such as this is concerned) seems to be only complexity. Just to clarify what I'm saying (or, more specifically, what I'm not saying) here: I am absolutely **not** trying to start some antidatabase revolution and revert everyone to writing to text files again. However, ultimately, the **most important** thing that any database does for you is to persist your changes to disk. As a result, we're just cutting out the middleman.

To the second point of why you *shouldn't* follow this idea when designing your system: obviously, all of the RDBMS out there offer many more features – although persisting data is the **most** important feature, managing concurrency comes in a very close second, and our solution will not do that very well, nor will it provide any form of indexing, backup capabilities, transaction control, or any of the other features that database systems have offered for decades.

Save

Let's look at the method that will persist the changes (Listing 2-4).

Listing 2-4. Code – CashDesk.Server/Persistence/PersistData.cs

```
public void Save<TDataEvent, TEvent>(TEventStreamBase eventStream)
            where TDataEvent : IDataEvent, new()
            where TEvent : IEvent
{
    var changes = eventStream.Changes;
    if (changes == null || !changes.Any())
    {
        return;
    }

    var dataStream = new List<TDataEvent>();
    foreach (var change in changes)
    {
        var eventChange = (TEvent)change;
        if (!eventChange.IsNew) continue;

        var dataEvent = new TDataEvent()
        {
            Transaction = eventChange.Transaction,
            EventType = typeof(TDataEvent).AssemblyQualifiedName
        };
        dataStream.Add(dataEvent);
    }
    var saveChanges = new SaveChanges()
    {
        Changes = dataStream.Select(a => (object)a).ToList(),
        StreamName = eventStream.StreamName
    };

    var dataStreamSerialised = JsonConvert.SerializeObject(saveChanges);

    _dataEvents.Append(eventStream.StreamName, dataStreamSerialised);
}
```

We should probably start by addressing the elephant in the room: this code does not actually write anything to disk. In fact, the code to do that is in its own project, which we'll visit later on. If you chose to use this as a basis for persisting to a database, you would change the code there – not here. The **_dataEvents** property is an injected reference to this class.

Again, let's break the code down and see what's going on; the first thing to note is the method signature.

Listing 2-5. Code – CashDesk.Server/Persistence/PersistData.cs

```
public void Save<TDataEvent, TEvent>(TEventStreamBase eventStream)
        where TDataEvent : IDataEvent, new()
        where TEvent : IEvent
```

If you're not familiar with .Net, the code in Listing 2-5 may look a little strange; however, all we're doing here is accepting three parameters to the method: two types, **TDataEvent** and **TEvent**, and an **eventStream**. The **where** clauses are simply telling the compiler that the types that we're given must conform to a certain criterion (e.g., TDataEvent must be of a type that implements the interface **IDataEvent**, and it must be possible to construct the type).

In fact, because we're only dealing with a single entity type, this is probably unnecessary; however, I thought that it would be good to have a base from which to expand this project.

The next section of code (Listing 2-6) deals with traversing the list of changes.

Listing 2-6. Code – CashDesk.Server/Persistence/PersistData.cs

```
var changes = eventStream.Changes;
if (changes == null || !changes.Any())
{
    return;
}

var dataStream = new List<TDataEvent>();
foreach (var change in changes)
{
    var eventChange = (TEvent)change;
    if (!eventChange.IsNew) continue;
```

```
    var dataEvent = new TDataEvent()
    {
        Transaction = eventChange.Transaction,
        EventType = typeof(TDataEvent).AssemblyQualifiedName
    };
    dataStream.Add(dataEvent);
}
```

Listing 2-6 starts with a simple gated check – if there are no changes, then do nothing. Following that, we create a new collection and begin to add any changes to it that are new; that is, they have been made since the data was read. For each change, we store the transaction itself and a reference to the data type of that transaction.

Listing 2-7. Code – CashDesk.Server/Persistence/PersistData.cs

```
var saveChanges = new SaveChanges()
{
    Changes = dataStream.Select(a => (object)a).ToList(),
    StreamName = eventStream.StreamName
};
var dataStreamSerialised = JsonConvert.SerializeObject(saveChanges);
_dataEvents.Append(eventStream.StreamName, dataStreamSerialised);
```

Finally, in Listing 2-7, we create a new class, **SaveChanges**, which is then serialized, and then we pass control over to **_dataEvents**, to add our serialized class to the persisted data on disk.

The *Append* method on the *_dataEvents* class, as I said earlier, can pretty much do whatever it likes (it is the responsibility of that class to actually save the data), although we will make a slight assumption in the *Load* method.

Load

Again, for the *Load* method, let's see the full method initially, and then we can dissect it.

Listing 2-8. Code – CashDesk.Server/Persistence/PersistData.cs

```
public TEventStreamBase Load(string streamName)
{
    var dataEventsSerialised = _dataEvents.Read(streamName);
    var dataEvents = new List<TEventStreamBase>();

    foreach (var dataEventSerialised in dataEventsSerialised)
    {
        var dataEvent = JsonConvert.DeserializeObject<SaveChanges>
        (dataEventSerialised);
        dataEvents.Add(new TEventStreamBase()
        {
            Changes = dataEvent.Changes,
            StreamName = dataEvent.StreamName
        });
    }

    if (dataEvents == null || !dataEvents.Any()
        || (!dataEvents.Where(a => a?.Changes?.Any() ?? false)?.Any()
            ?? false))
    {
        var newStream = new TEventStreamBase()
        {
            StreamName = streamName
        };

        return newStream;
    }

    var eventStream = new TEventStreamBase()
    {
        StreamName = dataEvents.First().StreamName
    };
```

```
    foreach (var dataEvent in dataEvents)
    {
        foreach (var eachEvent in dataEvent.Changes)
        {
            var obj = JObject.Parse(eachEvent.ToString());
            var eventType = obj["EventType"].Value<string>();
            var type = Type.GetType(eventType);

            if (type == typeof(DataCashDeskTransactionAddedEvent))
            {
                var settings = new JsonSerializerSettings();
                settings.Converters.Add(new
                CashDeskTransactionConverter());

                var deserialisedObject = JsonConvert.
                DeserializeObject(eachEvent.ToString(), type, settings);

                eventStream.Apply(deserialisedObject);
            }
        }
    }
    return eventStream;
}
```

The signature of the Load method is very straight-forward (Listing 2-9).

Listing 2-9. Code – CashDesk.Server/Persistence/PersistData.cs

```
public TEventStreamBase Load(string streamName)
```

As we can see in Listing 2-9, all we're doing here is accepting a stream name and returning a **TEventStreamBase** (the class itself accepts a generic type that determines what this is). In our case, this will return a **CashDeskEventStream**.

The next stage is to simply read and deserialize the data.

Listing 2-10. Code – CashDesk.Server/Persistence/PersistData.cs

```
var dataEventsSerialised = _dataEvents.Read(streamName);
var dataEvents = new List<TEventStreamBase>();

foreach (var dataEventSerialised in dataEventsSerialised)
{
    var dataEvent = JsonConvert.DeserializeObject<SaveChanges>
    (dataEventSerialised);
    dataEvents.Add(new TEventStreamBase()
    {
        Changes = dataEvent.Changes,
        StreamName = dataEvent.StreamName
    });
}

if (dataEvents == null || !dataEvents.Any()
    || (!dataEvents.Where(a => a?.Changes?.Any() ?? false)?.Any()
        ?? false))
{
    var newStream = new TEventStreamBase()
    {
        StreamName = streamName
    };

    return newStream;
}
```

Listing 2-10 starts with a call to *_dataEvents.Read(streamName)*. This method (which we will see shortly) returns an array of strings. That is, we expect to get more than one value back. The reason for this is that as the data is written in a staggered fashion, we should expect it to be read in the same way.

Note   While this approach fits well for reading and writing to a series of text files, or even to a NoSQL database, it perhaps fits less well in a relational database such as Microsoft SQL Server or Oracle; having said that, it could be argued that the very concept of event sourcing sits less well with those databases.

Following the deserialization of the data into a series of events, we then have a gated check to ensure that we actually have something to load. The next section of code simply rebuilds those events.

Listing 2-11. Code – CashDesk.Server/Persistence/PersistData.cs

```
foreach (var dataEvent in dataEvents)
{
    foreach (var eachEvent in dataEvent.Changes)
    {
        var obj = JObject.Parse(eachEvent.ToString());
        var eventType = obj["EventType"].Value<string>();
        var type = Type.GetType(eventType);

        if (type == typeof(DataCashDeskTransactionAddedEvent))
        {
            var settings = new JsonSerializerSettings();
            settings.Converters.Add(new CashDeskTransactionConverter());

            var deserialisedObject = JsonConvert.
            DeserializeObject(eachEvent.ToString(), type, settings);

            eventStream.Apply(deserialisedObject);
        }
    }
}
return eventStream;
```

In Listing 2-11, we can see that each event is being loaded into memory, and the **Apply** method is being called in order to reapply any logic behind the creation of the event. This part is important, as the event stream must be loaded back into memory in exactly the same state that it was in before it was saved.

> **Note**   Event sourcing provides an unseen benefit in this regard: if you change your code, it is possible, in an event-sourced system, to re-run every event that has ever occurred on your system since it began. This kind of automated acceptance testing would be very difficult and time-consuming to implement in a normal state-based system but comes for free with event sourcing.

I won't go into the details of the serialization custom converter, as it's a quirk of the serialization library that I've used inside .Net. If you're interested in this, then I've left a link to a blog post in the code on GitHub for further details.

Before we proceed, let's see the *DataPersistence* project.

Writing to Files

Let's now see how we're actually writing and reading to the file system. This is for completeness, as it really makes very little difference to the architecture how the data is persisted.

Listing 2-12.   Code – CashDesk.DataPersistence/DataEventsPersistence.cs

```
public void Append(string streamName, string dataStream)
{
    if (!Directory.Exists("data"))
    {
        Directory.CreateDirectory("data");
    }

    string fileName = $"data/{DateTime.UtcNow.ToString("yyyy-MM-dd-hh-mm-
ss")}-{streamName}";

    using var file = new StreamWriter(fileName, true);
    file.Write(dataStream);
}
```

Listing 2-12 is the **Append** method. It simply creates a new file with a date/time stamp in the file name, along with the stream name, and writes that out.

Finally, we come to the Read method.

Listing 2-13. Code – CashDesk.DataPersistence/DataEventsPersistence.cs

```
public string[] Read(string streamName)
{
    if (!Directory.Exists("data"))
    {
        return new[] { string.Empty };
    }

    List<string> returnList = new List<string>();

    foreach (var file in Directory.GetFiles("data"))
    {
        if (!file.Contains(streamName))
            continue;

        string streamText = File.ReadAllText(file);
        returnList.Add(streamText);
    }

    return returnList.OrderBy(a => a).ToArray();
}
```

Again, Listing 2-13 doesn't contain anything particularly interesting; we simply read all of the files in the directory that contain the specified stream name and return that list in order of the date.

Summary

Event sourcing provides us with many benefits out of the box: the ability to reconstruct the state of the system from its formative events; the ability to go back to any given time within the history of the system and see the exact state at that time; it even provides an additional avenue for testing, given that any change to the system can be checked against everything that has ever happened to the system.

We discussed the difference between event sourcing and auditing and how to deal with a system where the events can't change.

Projections provide a way for us to view the data in the system, and snapshots give us a mechanism to roll-up of a set of events for a given period in order that we are not obliged to re-read them each time.

CQRS, while not the sole focus of this chapter, also provides a number of benefits in its own right. You get a massively increased speed for reading and writing data – although you do sacrifice immediate consistency.

CHAPTER 3

The Travel Agent Problem

Travel agents started around the end of the 19th century. The idea being that they would organize your holiday for you and, in return, they would take a fee for doing so. A modern travel agent will organize flights (some even have their own airlines), book hotels or accommodation, arrange transport to and from the airport, and offer excursions and trips.

Note   I'm writing this in a unique time. I live in the UK, and the country, and indeed the world, has been thrown into turmoil by a pandemic, the like of which hasn't been seen for 100 years! This is a relevant point because the subject of this particular chapter has been especially hard hit by the measures taken to control the virus. I intend, in no way, to make light of this situation; however, a travel agency is an excellent example of a distributed transaction, and so I decided to keep the case study as is.

When you ask a travel agent to book a holiday, you would expect them to inform you that they had successfully booked the holiday on your behalf or that the dates that you requested were not available. You would not expect to be informed that they had booked the flight and transfer from the airport, yet the hotel was full that week; you would expect the system to check all the systems for availability, and to either book all the requested services, or none of them.

© Paul Michaels 2022
P. Michaels, *Software Architecture by Example*, https://doi.org/10.1007/978-1-4842-7990-8_3

In this chapter, we will investigate a system such as may be found at a travel agent – that is, where multiple third-party external systems must work together. We will investigate how to create a distributed transaction across multiple services.

Background

Lunar Polly Travel has submitted a brief for us to design a system for their brand-new travel agency. They wish to sell trips to the moon, and they are partnering with a well-known space travel company to do so.

The system is currently expected to be low volume; however, they hope that demand will rapidly increase, as people get used to the idea of space travel.

The company had recruited a well-respected and well-known figure within the travel industry as the managing director of this new firm. You have spoken to the managing director of this new company, and he has given you a list of high-level requirements. Let's see, in details, what the requirements are.

Requirements

Unlike in previous chapters, in this situation, we are dealing with a company that does not exist yet. While the managing director may be an expert in his field, there is no existing system to model the new one on – not even a manual system. This is a factor that should be carefully considered – while the person describing the requirements may know the industry (in this case, that's not even likely, as it's a new industry), he may not know the specific challenges faced by the staff, the customers, or the vendors.

Just to be clear, what I'm saying here is **not** that you should only ever accept jobs in well-known industries, with well-trodden paths; what I'm saying is that you should ensure that the software design can cope with whatever scenarios you can consider. A good method of doing that is to design the customer journey and then play it through with someone else.

Note   I am personally not an expert in any of the industries mentioned in this book. That statement, obviously, goes double for the industry of space tourism! The problems that I've created are for the purpose of demonstrating potential solutions, which can be applicable cross-industry.

Having spoken to the MD, the high-level requirements that you agree on are the following:

- Must be able to book a space flight.

- Book a hospital check before the launch.

- Book a hotel on the night before the launch.

- If any of the bookings can't be made, then none can be made (there's little point in a hotel room if the flight is cancelled).

- The system must be able to scale massively, as the MD expects the demand to grow exponentially.

All of the systems have a public API that we can query, and use to book the relevant resource. Each one of the providers has offered to work with us to get this running and so are willing to change their APIs or systems within reason.

Let's consider how we could achieve this solution.

Options

The central issue here is that of a transaction. Actually building a system to call these APIs is trivial; however, we have an issue with ensuring that we either book all or none of the selected services.

We also have an issue with scaling – while it may be trivial to call the APIs, we should consider what would happen if we were to get two conflicting bookings: if we book a flight for person A and a hotel for person B and then try to book the flight for person B, we'll find that we've already used that booking up for someone else.

Manual Process

As with previous chapters, let's investigate how we could achieve this through a manual process to help us better understand the business domain.

We can imagine that, if an order for a space flight were to come in, the process would be relatively straightforward; the sales assistant would:

1. Contact the space flight provider to book the flight itself.

2. Phone the hospital to book the pre- and postcheck.

3. Ring the hotel to book a room for the night before the launch.

That seems a very easy process; however, what would we do if at stage 2, the sales assistant found out that the hospital was too busy on that day? Well, in that case, we would try to cancel the space flight.

Should we have a similar problem with the hotel, then we would need to cancel the two bookings.

Another possible way to approach this would be as follows:

1. Phone the space shuttle company and ask them to reserve the day that we wish to book.

2. Contact the hospital and do the same.

3. Ask the hotel to reserve a room for that night.

Then, if any of these are unavailable, we could get back to the others and ask them to cancel the reservation; otherwise, we could book each service.

This looks like a much better system, but let's put ourselves in the position of, say, the hospital; they are busy and are essentially tying up one of their bookings until we get back to them; they potentially would need to turn away other bookings for that day, as a result; similarly with the space shuttle company – although the costs involved for the space shuttle company are much larger.

The process that we're discussing here in various forms is a **transaction**.

Transactions

Let's discuss exactly what a transaction is with relation to data. Essentially, a transaction is a single unit of work; typically, it will combine more than one activity. Let's take the following example of transferring some money from one bank account to another:

1. Account 1: Debit £300.00

2. Account 2: Credit £300.00

If I contact my bank and ask them to transfer this money, the preceding process is a simplified version of what happens: they take the money out of one account, and they put it in another – a two-stage process. Now, what would happen if in between 1 and 2, the system crashed? Without a transaction to wrap around these two activities, **Account 1** would still be debited, but the money would simply disappear – it would never make it to **Account 2**.

A transaction around the two activities ensures that either all of these activities happen, or none do. The valid result states are either the transaction failed and **Account 1** still has the £300, or the transaction succeeded and **Account 2** now has that money, but **Account 1** does not. In order to ensure the validity of this data, most database systems implement a concept of an **ACID** transaction.

ACID

ACID is, in fact, an acronym; it stands for Atomic, Consistent, Isolated, and Durable.

> **Note**   This may seem like a divergence from the subject in hand, but as with many such things in computer science, new problems have typically already been solved years ago, but in a different environment.

I won't delve into every tenet in detail, although the concepts are very straightforward.

Atomic

We've already seen what **atomicity** means: it guarantees that all parts of a transaction either succeed or fail.

Consistent

Consistency is concerned with the integrity of your data – this means different things depending on the database, but let's imagine that we have a sales order and sales order lines; assuming the database was set up such that they were linked in a primary / foreign key relationship, it would not adhere to the rule of **Consistency** if the sales order record were allowed to be removed, but the lines left orphaned in the database.

Isolation

In fact, the principle of **isolation** is the one that we are primarily concerned with here: this relates to concurrency. That is, what happens if transactions or operations are executed at the same time. The rule here is deceptively simple: where operations occur concurrently, the database should be left in the same end state as if the transactions were executed sequentially.

In order to explain this, an example is useful; let's return to our bank transaction, but this time, we have two:

Transaction 1		Transaction 2
Account 1	Debit £300	Print Account 1
Account 2	Credit £300	Print Account 2

Note   Transaction 2 does not make any changes to the database. This is still a valid transaction (in SQL databases, this would be a **SELECT** statement).

We'll assume a starting balance of £500 in account 1 and account 2.

Remember that the key thing here is that despite executing at the same time, the end state of the database must be the same as executing the transactions sequentially. There are two ways that these can be executed sequentially (I'll shorten to using T1 or T2 for the sake of brevity):

T1, T2 = £200 in account 1, £800 in account 2

T2, T1 = £500 in account 1, £500 in account 2

There are no other valid states here; that is, there is no other sequence in which we could execute these two transactions.

Note   This is clearly an oversimplified example; in a real database system, you may find dozens or even hundreds of transactions executing concurrently; however, the same rule applies for isolation.

Let's investigate how these transactions could execute concurrently in a way that might threaten this state. To make this easier, we'll label the points of the transactions (the empty lines are there for a reason, which will become clear shortly):

	Transaction 1		**Transaction 2**
1	Account 1	Debit £300	Print Account 1
2			
3	Account 2	Credit £300	Print Account 2
4			

Let's imagine that the transactions execute in the following manner:

T1: 1, 2

T2: 1, 2, 3, 4

T1: 3, 4

In this example, what should T2 print? **Account 1** has now had £300 deducted, but **Account 2** has not been credited; the output here would be

> **Account 1**: £200
>
> **Account 2**: £500

If we look back at our list of valid states – this is neither, and so this path of execution would not be considered isolated.

Note   Some databases actually provide a facility for you to breach isolation in just this way; it's generally termed a *dirty read* and essentially allows you to look at uncommitted data.

Another situation to consider would be the following:

> T2: 1, 2
>
> T1: 1, 2, 3, 4
>
> T1: 3, 4

In this example, T2 may print

> **Account 1**: £500
>
> **Account 2**: £800

Again, this is not one of the valid states that we listed earlier. Finally, we should consider what would happen if T1 were to crash at point 2 – this could leave the database in a situation where not only were the values displayed incorrectly but that (as we stated earlier) the money has disappeared.

Durable

Finally, we have durability; arguably, without this, there's little purpose in a database. Essentially, it means that once you've committed some data to a database, it remains there.

Note   In Chapter 2, we discussed the principle of event sourcing. If you consider that this method never actually changes data at all, then you are effectively dealing with a different data set for each transaction – meaning that any event-sourced system is, by definition, ACID compliant.

Now that we understand what a transaction is, we should see if we can apply this to our scenario; because we're dealing with disparate systems as part of our transaction, what we're actually talking about is a **distributed transaction**.

Distributed Transactions

A distributed transaction is a method to provide the functionality that we expect from a standard transaction across multiple systems. Let's see how that works and whether it meets our requirements.

The main principle here is, what is known as, a two-phase commit; this is exactly what it sounds like: you first announce your intent to commit, and then commit. A distributed transaction across **n** systems would have **n + 1** participants. In our case, we have three systems, and therefore, we have four participants.

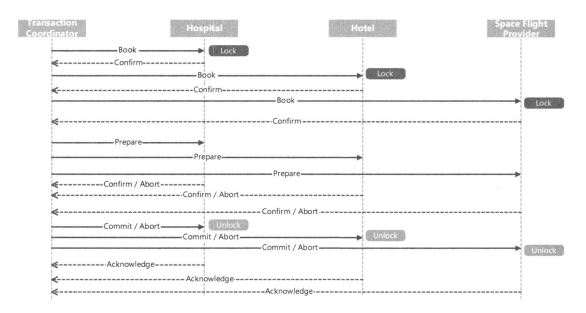

Figure 3-1. *Sequence diagram*

Figure 3-1 illustrates the sequence flow for a distributed transaction. The transaction coordinator essentially polls each participant in the transaction and *asks* if they are ready to begin the transaction. If the coordinator receives a confirmation from every participant, then it issues a commit instruction and, again, expects each participant to confirm that they have committed.

Each participant in this transaction is required to keep a persisted state of the transaction following the lock, until the data is committed, or an abort message is sent. The coordinator would need to persist the state of the transaction after the first commit is sent; this would repeatedly poll the participants until it receives an acknowledgment.

The transaction in the diagram would have a unique reference, which would be distributed during the initial message. From this point on, any communication would refer to this reference.

This seems an eminently usable system; admittedly, it's a little chatty and likely slow, but we have a guarantee that all the bookings are made, or none are made. However, we should consider how this system deals with failure.

The rules here are as follows:

- If a participant receives a message for a transaction that it wasn't aware of, it should abort, unless it's a commit message – in which case, it should acknowledge (without committing).

- Participants must persist the transaction state between locking to unlocking.

- Once a participant has *confirmed* in response to a *prepare*, it must wait for a commit or an abort.

Let's consider some possible scenarios.

Possible Scenarios

The hospital has no available appointments on that day

1. The coordinator sends a message to the hospital but receives an error back, indicating the booking isn't available.

2. Locks are released.

The space flight provider's system crashes after receiving a prepare message but before responding

1. Book messages are sent to all participants, and confirmations received.

2. Prepare is send to all participants.

3. Confirmations are received from the hospital and the hotel.

4. After a period of time, the transaction coordinator times out the transaction, and abort messages are issued to all participants.

5. When the space flight provider's system comes back online, it reads the persisted log of the transaction and replies to the prepare with a confirm.

6. The transaction coordinator now knows nothing of the transaction, as the persisted log is deleted, and so it sends an abort.

The hotel's system crashes after receiving a commit message and committing the transaction but before acknowledging

1. All the initial messages are sent and confirmed.

2. Prepare messages are sent and confirmed.

3. Commit messages are sent to all participants, and acknowledgments are received from both the space flight and hospital systems.

4. The transaction coordinator continues to send commit messages to the hotel system.

5. When the hotel system comes back online, it has already committed and removed the log of the transaction, so when it receives a commit message, it simply replies with an acknowledgment.

The transaction coordinator crashes after sending all the prepare messages but before receiving any confirmations

1. All the initial messages are sent and confirmed.

2. All the prepare messages are sent.

3. The participants all reply to the prepare message with a confirmation.

4. Since the coordinator is now down, it cannot issue a commit message; however, the participants have confirmed the prepare, and so they must await a commit or abort message; no timeout is possible in this case, as no single participant can know the state of the rest.

As we can see from the preceding examples, the final one presents a real problem. It is unlikely that the hotel, for example, would be willing to commit to a system that would indefinitely lock their internal system, and so because of this, a distributed two-phase transaction is not practical for this problem.

Although a distributed transaction is not possible, we can certainly use some elements from that system to inform our choice.

Distributed Transaction with Timeout

We could easily adapt our distributed transaction to do this by simply changing the rules slightly. We could allow the participants in the transaction to unilaterally time out – for example, when a prepare message has been issued, but no commit received. We could then have an error state where the transaction coordinator polled all of the participants at the end to determine the status of the booking. Where one or more of the participants have not secured the booking, we simply attempt to book; if we can't, then cancel the others.

In Figure 3-2, any of the services can unilaterally decide that they wish to time out during the timeout window. During this time, should they decide to time out, they would issue a message to the controller, who would then bear the responsibility of clean up.

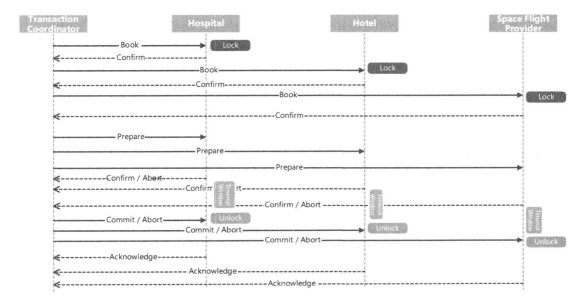

Figure 3-2. *Distributed Transaction Sequence Diagram*

In this case, clean-up is, effectively, attempting to cancel the remaining transactions: if a **confirm** hasn't been issued, then by abandoning the transaction; or, where it has, then by instigating a cancellation.

Book and Cancel

Our next option is a little less from a computer science background and more from a business background. We could simply book the resources and, where a single element of the booking is not available, attempt to cancel the other parts. The obvious risk here is that we would not be able to cancel a particular thing; for example, the hotel may refuse the cancellation.

Note   Having spoken to people that have faced this issue in the travel industry, this is not only common practice, but it is not unheard of for this transaction to be referred to a call center for them to manually correct the booking.

Hold a Booking

This possibility appears at first glance to be the most sensible. Here, we are effectively saying to the service provider that we wish them to reserve a place for us, but not to actually make the booking. We have discussed this kind of scenario previously in this chapter. The issue here is that you are asking a provider to potentially refuse a firm booking in exchange for your potential one. In fact, this could be said to fit into our transaction diagram shown before – we need simply to accept the ***prepare*** as a hold instruction and ***confirm*** as a firm booking.

Advanced Purchase

This appears to be the approach taken by the bigger players in the travel industry today. Again, it is also not a technical solution to the problem, but a business one. What you do is project how many trips you are likely to sell and then buy that many from the supplier. In our case, we may decide to buy 20 nights in the hotel and book and pre-pay for 20 hospital appointments on the same day. However, in our case, it would not be practical for a simple reason: the space shuttle flight would be prohibitively expensive.

Note   At the time of writing, NASA was paying SpaceX around $55 million per astronaut for a place on a shuttle. The average price for an international flight on an airplane was around $1,300.

Consequently, this is unlikely to be the best decision (given that only one flight not being re-sold could potentially bankrupt the company).

Business Decision

In fact, as with many such cases, the right answer here is not an architectural one, but a business one. The person making such a decision is going to need to balance risk against potential profit; such decisions are beyond the scope of this book, safe to say that it is very unlikely that you will face any architectural problem that doesn't contain an element of a business decision.

Having spoken to a representative from the business, they decide to adopt the *Book and Cancel* option.

Target Architecture

Now that we have established how we will interface with the various providers, we should also consider how we can make this scalable, and what the system will look like.

Note   We have already indicated that space travel is so expensive that it is probably currently limited to (at most) a few thousand people in the world; however, that doesn't mean that it will always be so – when cars first came out, they were exclusively for the wealthy enthusiast, but today (at least, at the time of writing), they are so prevalent that car crash injuries are the eighth leading cause of death in the world.

In addition to using a (form of) distributed transaction, we need to be able to execute many transactions synchronously. As with previous chapters, in this situation, we come back to a message broker. Each individual booking must be made synchronously. Given that we intend to cancel if the booking is not successful, the order that we should do these things is important.

Figure 3-3 shows that we start by booking based on the least risk. This diagram would work in conjunction with the distributed transaction before but better illustrates the process.

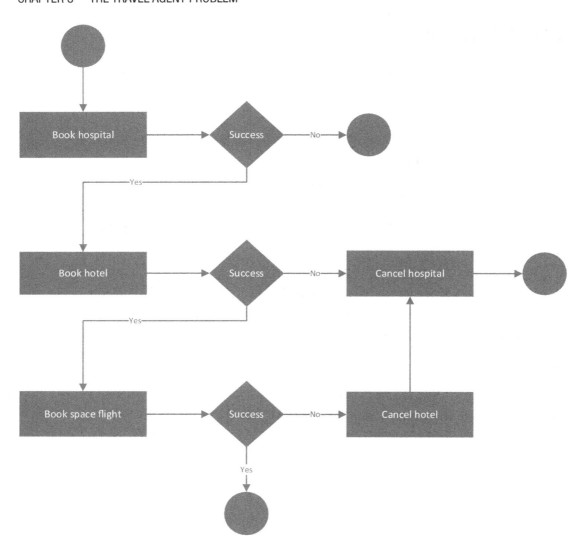

Figure 3-3. *Logical flow*

After establishing what the flow of the booking will look like, we should consider what will execute this. We've discussed that this would need to be scalable, and we've also considered that it would need to occur in order. There are a number of ways to achieve this.

Based on our earlier diagrams, we need to establish how we will represent the different parts of the transaction. Only the transaction coordinator falls within our domain (although as with previous chapters, the third-party systems will be emulated by us).

Stateful Service

One possibility here is to start to make the bookings and to persist the state of the booking. That is, each time a part of the transaction executes, a flag would be updated in some form of persistence layer. If the service were to crash then, when it came back up, it would check the persisted state and resume where it left off – as described in the earlier section on distributed transactions.

This service itself could then execute based on a message broker, but the responsibility for persistence is within the service. This has the advantage of meaning that the service could be taken and deployed anywhere (as it's self-contained). However, it does mean that each individual transaction must be managed by a single instance of the coordinator.

Distributed Service

This option would use the message broker itself as a persistence layer. The way that this works is that the service behaves very much as before but simply writes a message back to a queue, and then another instance of the same service picks that up. The advantage here is that the service is more scalable, as a new instance is used for each section of the task. This means that we can increase the number of workers and the new workers will pick up the next part of the transaction.

Target Architecture Diagram

We've now covered the principles of a distributed transaction and discussed how we might implement this.

Figure 3-4 shows the target architecture. Essentially, we're leveraging the message broker in order to orchestrate the transaction coordinator. Each time a transaction is started, then a message is added to the queue to communicate with the hospital API; when we have a successful response, then we'll communicate with the hotel API and so forth. Each time a step in the transaction is completed, we add a message to the broker; that way, should the transaction coordinator itself fail, we would simply come back up and read the relevant message queue.

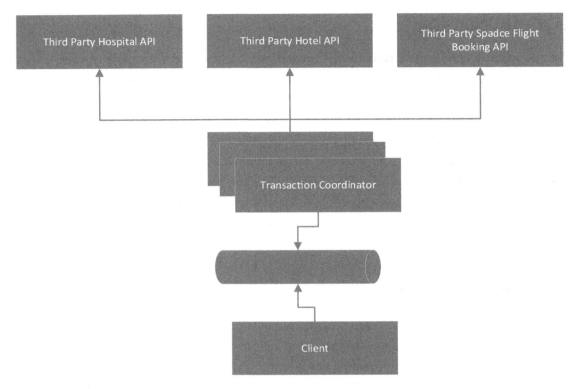

Figure 3-4. *Target architecture*

Examples

In the example here, we're going to create three APIs. Since the Tech Appendix for Chapter 1 covers creating APIs in .Net, I will not re-cover that here. Save to say that we will have three APIs.

As you will be familiar with by now, the code for this will be in the following GitHub repository:

```
https://github.com/Apress/software-architecture-by-example
```

Project Structure

Our sample solution will consist of three parts: third-party APIs, a client, and a coordinator.

Figure 3-5 illustrates the project structure for our sample. Each third-party service is represented by an API project. In our example, we've made them all broadly REST

APIs; however, that is by no means a prerequisite. In fact, since these represent APIs that we have little control over, the code to interact with them should be segregated and abstracted where feasible (we haven't really done that here, as that is not the purpose of this example).

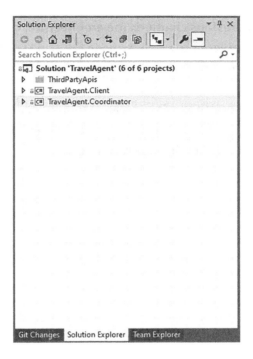

Figure 3-5. *Project structure*

Before we go about creating the rest of the project, we will need to set up the Azure Service Bus. I've covered setting this up via the Azure Portal (`https://portal.azure. com`); in order to follow along, you'll need to have an Azure account.

Note   At the time of writing, Microsoft was offering a 12-month free Azure subscription.

Service Bus Configuration

Although we are using Azure in this example, you could easily substitute any other cloud provider message broker or any message broker at all – for example, **RabbitMQ** would work fine for this situation.

As we've discussed in previous chapters, the architectural decision to make here is whether to use a cloud provider or to try to manage the scale yourself. This particular example – low traffic now, but an expectation to ramp up rapidly – lends itself very well to the cloud model.

The first step in Azure Service Bus is to create a *namespace*.

In Figure 3-6, we are creating a namespace for our Service Bus. This is effectively a grouping mechanism for all the Service Bus resources.

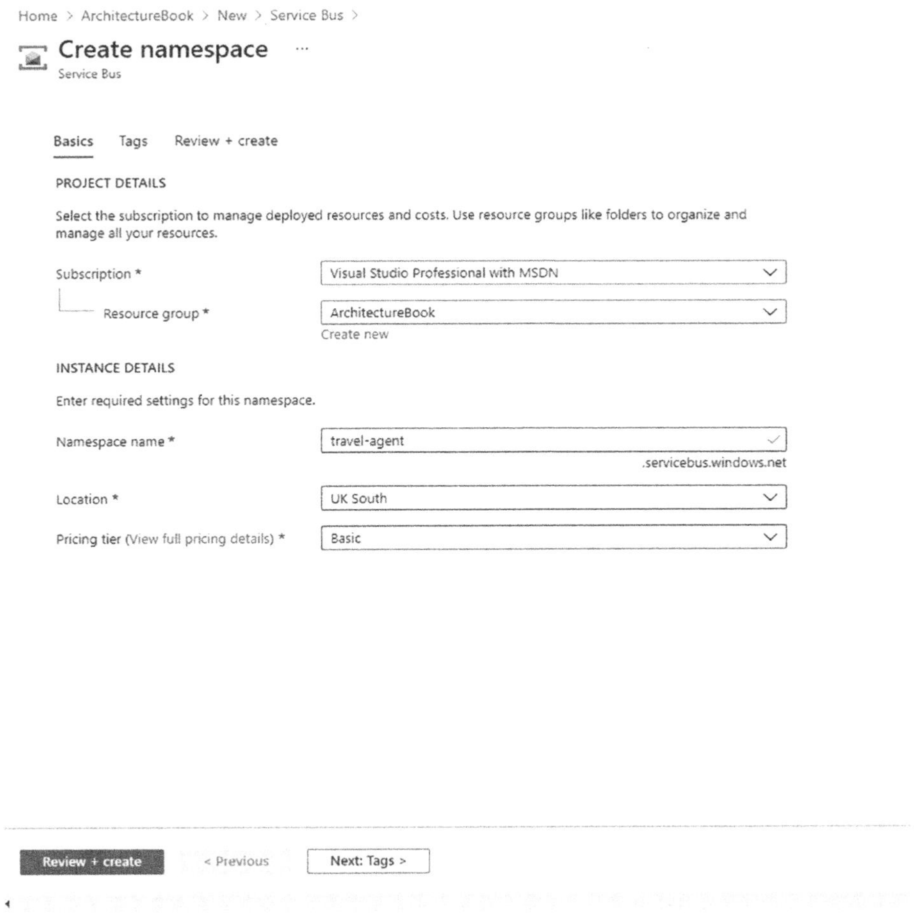

Home > ArchitectureBook > New > Service Bus >

Create namespace   ...
Service Bus

Basics   Tags   Review + create

PROJECT DETAILS

Select the subscription to manage deployed resources and costs. Use resource groups like folders to organize and manage all your resources.

Subscription * | Visual Studio Professional with MSDN   ∨ |

└──── Resource group * | ArchitectureBook   ∨ |
                                    Create new

INSTANCE DETAILS

Enter required settings for this namespace.

Namespace name * | travel-agent   ✓ |
                                                              .servicebus.windows.net

Location * | UK South   ∨ |

Pricing tier (View full pricing details) * | Basic   ∨ |

Review + create   < Previous   Next: Tags >

Figure 3-6. *Create namespace*

Within the namespace, we can create *Queues* and *Topics*.

For our example, we will create a single queue, from which we will orchestrate everything. Figure 3-7 illustrates how to set up the queue; however, there are other ways to do this. For example, we could generate a queue for each section of the transaction.

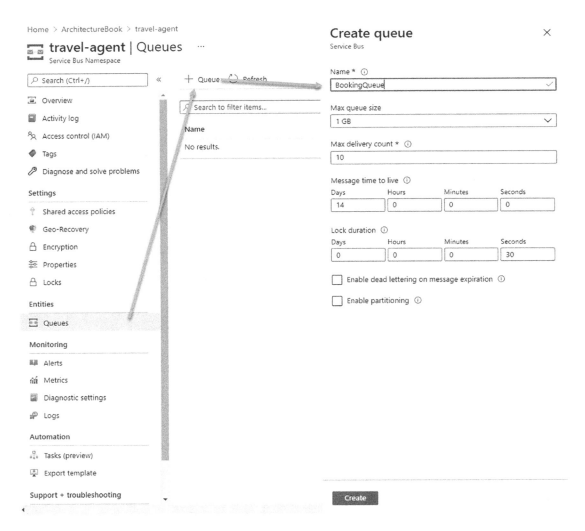

Figure 3-7. *Create a queue*

The next step is to generate an *access policy*.

In order to connect to the Service Bus, we need to configure an access policy (shown in Figure 3-8). This allows us to dictate what permissions are given to processes that connect to the Service Bus. In our case, we have an access policy on our *queue* and an access policy for the *namespace*. You should always attempt to allocate the least privilege to any resource; in our case, that's the ability to read and write to the queue, but not to affect the queue (i.e., delete or change).

Figure 3-8. *Access policy*

Now that we have successfully configured our service bus, we can move onto the main part of the project; this is our coordinator.

Coordinator

The coordinator here will simply listen to the Service Bus queue that we've created (*BookingQueue*) and will process each message by its type. The coordinator holds absolutely no state, which means that we can run several of these processes should we encounter a rush in orders.

Our coordinator code essentially does two things: it processes incoming messages, and it calls the third-party APIs. I would encourage the reader to check out the source code, as I have intentionally made it verbose in order to aid readability. If we think back to the logic in Figure 3-3, there are a list of endpoints to contact, and this is where we'll start in the code.

Listing 3-1. BookingRequestHandler.cs

```
public BookingRequestHandler(string connectionString, IHttpClientFactory
httpClientFactory)
{
_connectionString = connectionString;
_httpClientFactory = httpClientFactory;

    _endPoints = new LinkedList<string>();
    _endPoints.AddLast(BOOKING_REQUEST);
    _endPoints.AddLast(BOOK_HOSPITAL);
    _endPoints.AddLast(BOOK_HOTEL);
    _endPoints.AddLast(BOOK_SPACEFLIGHT);
    _endPoints.AddLast(BOOKING_COMPLETED);
}
```

In Listing 3-1, what we are doing is leveraging the C# *LinkedList* in order to chain together these endpoints.

Note   Although this structure is specific to C#, the concept of a Linked List is certainly not. If you are using a different language, there is almost certainly an equivalent; and if there is not, creating a linked list is a trivial exercise.

The next stage is to handle the request itself. In *Program.cs,* you will see some code that registers an event handler for receiving a message. The code for that handler is in the *BookingRequestHandler.cs.*

Listing 3-2. BookingRequestHandler.cs

```
        public async Task ProcessBookingRequest(string type, DateTime date,
        string function)
        {
            var node = _endPoints.Find(type);

            switch (type)
```

```
    {
        case "BookingRequest":
            if (function == FUNCTION_BOOK)
            {
                Console.WriteLine("Booking Request");
                await SendMessage(_connectionString, node.Next.
                Value, date, function);
            }
            else if (function == FUNCTION_CANCEL)
            {
                Console.WriteLine("Booking Request Failed and
                Successfully Cancelled");
            }
            break;

        case "BookHospital":
            await CallBookHospital(date, function, node);

            break;

        case "BookHotel":
            await CallBookHotel(date, function, node);

            break;

        case "BookSpaceFlight":
            await CallBookSpaceFlight(date, function, node);

            break;
    }

}
```

In Listing 3-2, we simply detect the type of request; there are four types: the initial booking request initiated by the client, and then the hospital booking request, hotel booking request, and space flight booking request – which are all initiated by the coordinator itself.

You'll also see from this code that we have a concept of a *function*; this allows us to traverse through the stack of bookings but, where there has been an error, back again to cancel each in turn. Listing 3-2 shows the top level of this; that is, either the request has just started or it has tried and failed to make the booking.

Note   As stated earlier, we won't go into the specific code of the APIs, but each has a random chance of failing to successfully make the booking and also a random delay before responding, thereby simulating a slightly more real-world environment.

The calls to the APIs are broadly all the same, and they all use proxies to call the API.

Listing 3-3. BookingRequestHandler.cs

```
private async Task CallBookHospital(DateTime date, string function,
LinkedListNode<string> node)
{
        var hospitalProxy = new HospitalProxy(_httpClientFactory);

        if (function == FUNCTION_BOOK)
        {
            if (await hospitalProxy.CallHospitalApi(date))
            {
                Console.WriteLine("Successfully booked hospital room");
                await SendMessage(_connectionString, node.Next.Value, date,
                function);
            }
            else
            {
                Console.WriteLine("Unable to book hospital
                room.  Cancelling");
                await SendMessage(_connectionString, node.Previous.Value,
                date, FUNCTION_CANCEL);
            }
        }
        else if (function == FUNCTION_CANCEL)
```

```
    {
        if (await hospitalProxy.CancelHospitalBooking(date))
        {
            Console.WriteLine("Successfully cancelled hospital room");
        }
        else
        {
            Console.WriteLine("Unable to cancel hospital room");
        }
        await SendMessage(_connectionString, node.Previous.Value, date,
        function);
    }
}
```

From Listing 3-3, we can see that there are two basic logical flows within the method: either we are trying to **book** or we are trying to **cancel**. Within the logic to book, should the call fail, we initiate a cancel flow by simply sending a message back to the queue with the cancel function and to the **previous** entity in the linked list. This will then traverse back up the list until the top.

The **cancel** branch of the code attempts to cancel; and if it can't, it logs the error and continues on through the list.

Note   In Listing 3-3, you'll notice that we are instantiating the proxy dependency inside the method – which does, somewhat, negate the purpose of having a proxy. I felt that structuring the code this way would better illustrate the intent of the code, although I would strongly advise against this practice.

The hospital and hotel methods are basically the same, in that they both follow the same path; however, the space flight booking method differs slightly.

Listing 3-4. BookingRequestHandler.cs

```
private async Task CallBookSpaceFlight(DateTime date, string function,
LinkedListNode<string> node)
{
        var spaceflightProxy = new SpaceFlightProxy(_httpClientFactory);
```

```
        if (function == FUNCTION_BOOK)
        {
            if (await spaceflightProxy.CallSpaceFlightApi(date))
            {
                Console.WriteLine("Successfully booked space flight");
                await SendMessage(_connectionString, node.Next.Value, date,
                function);
            }
            else
            {
                Console.WriteLine("Unable to book space
                flight.  Cancelling...");
                await SendMessage(_connectionString, node.Previous.Value,
                date, FUNCTION_CANCEL);
            }
        }
        else
        {
            throw new Exception("Cannot cancel space flight");
        }
}
```

The method that books the space flight, shown in Listing 3-4, does not handle the *cancel* branch. The reason is that this is the top of the list, so it can never be called to cancel. We also established that cancelling this would be prohibitively expensive, and so it is only ever called once we have successfully booked the rest of the trip.

Summary

We've been to the moon and back in this chapter! Transactions, especially distributed transactions, are a complex and nuanced topic. Transactions are always a good thing for data integrity, but even for local transactions, there is a price to pay; a long running transaction will cause locking problems - extend that to a distributed transaction, and you make the same locking problem exponentially worse!

We've discussed how you can use a tool such as a message broker in order to coordinate a transaction – which prevents the need to have a separate transaction coordinator.

Business decisions are an inescapable factor of software architecture. There's little point in designing an architecture for a company that they simply don't have the budget for, nor should you discount requirements such as time to market in designing a system. It's worth remembering that what you're building needs to be used – otherwise you're wasting time and money in building it. Often, more than one technical solution will present itself to a given problem – when this happens, it is incumbent on the architect to explain the options to the business and to abide by the business decision.

Further to this, once a decision is made, it should ideally be documented. There are several ways to document a decision – for example, you could simply keep the email that you receive; however, I would encourage you to research the use of Architectural Decision Records (ADR) – which are a way of recording your decision in the code itself.

CHAPTER 4

The Social Media Problem

Social media has been around for longer than you might think. While still at school and long before anyone had even heard the term "Facebook" (linked to a website), I used to run a Bulletin Board System (or BBS). People would dial in to our house phone number, and they could access features in this system, which included such things as a "wall" – a term that is now familiar to anyone using Facebook and with a very similar idea. There was also a messaging network that allowed communication across other BBS, known as FidoNet (still running to this date).

While the BBS world was fun to be a part of, it was not a particularly scalable system, nor did it need to be; at my house, there was a single phone line, meaning that one person could access the board at a time (assuming no one was trying to use the phone to actually make a call – a limitation that frequently irked other members of my family). However, in recent years, social media has become much more popular.

© Paul Michaels 2022
P. Michaels, *Software Architecture by Example*, https://doi.org/10.1007/978-1-4842-7990-8_4

Note   At the time of writing, Facebook has almost 3 billion active users, Twitter around 350 million, and LinkedIn around 250 million.

In this chapter, we're going to explore methods of dealing with this kind of extreme scalability, along with the cost of such architectures.

Background

We have been asked by an existing company, *Get Moving*, to create a social media platform. *Get Moving* is an international leisure company, with a series of gyms spanning the globe; they also have a successful suite of apps that allow people to follow exercise classes remotely. They would like a social media platform that allows users to interact with other members of the brand (whether that be members of the gym or just people that use the app).

Get Moving has 300 locations worldwide, with a total close to 3M members across the globe. They also have a further 2M people using their apps. Having spoken to the marketing director, he feels that the launch of this social media platform will double that figure, and he expects some users to use the service on a daily basis.

Requirements

Having spoken to the managing director of *Get Moving*, you establish that the software should have the following features:

- Users should be able to post details of their workout along with a comment.

- Other users should be able to reply or comment on these status updates.

- There are no geographical restrictions on who can view the posts.

- Should be massively scalable (initially, they expect around 20,000 users, but as they roll this out to the gym users, they quickly expect that to reach around 1M active users).

- While they expect the updates to appear on the timeline of both the user that has posted the update and the user that has commented, this does not have to be instantaneous. Further, the order of comments is unimportant.

After further conversations, you come up with a wireframe example of what this might look like.

Note   Those readers familiar with privacy laws may notice an issue with these requirements. Since this chapter is not concerned with those specific issues (as important as they may be), I'm going to ignore them, as doing so better serves the illustration; however, should you be faced with such a situation, you should ensure that your system does adhere to whatever rules are in place in the locale of your target audience.

Options

This set of requirements is, in fact, quite unique. When you typically speak to a client about their requirements for a system, they will not mention *non-functional requirements*, such as scalability. The reason is that they will assume that whatever functionality they ask for will be scalable, reliable, usable, extensible, secure, accessible, and all the other things that, as a software architect, you need to explicitly consider. The reason for this is that most modern systems are almost all of those things, out of the box. Taking ASP.NET as an example (since our example code is in .Net), you can create an ASP.NET website that will, with zero lines of code, be secure, usable, extensible, and accessible; depending on how you deal with the hosting, it can also be very scalable.

As the person designing the system, it then falls to you to identify if these requirements involve sacrifices elsewhere. The devil is in the details. What exactly do we mean by *usable*? What does reliable mean? Does it mean that the system should have zero downtime? Exactly what, about the system, would need to be extensible: Do the users of the system require the ability to extend the system, or do we just mean that a change to the functionality is quick and easy?

In truth, when we go to extremes with any of these nonfunctional requirements, we often sacrifice others. Let's take making the system both usable and accessible as an example; should we need to make the system accessible to people with very poor eyesight, we may increase the size of controls and text, place fewer items on a screen, and perhaps incorporate some form of voice control; however, when you gave that system to a person with perfect eyesight, they may not describe the system as being usable.

In our case, the client has realized that their requirement of user numbers is not standard and therefore requires special mention. Our job at this stage is to highlight to them what, if anything, we would need to sacrifice in order to provide that scalability.

In previous chapters, we've approached the problem by first exploring what the system would look like without automation.

Manual Process

Admittedly, this scenario probably lends itself less to a manual process than any that we have discussed so far in this book; however, let's complete the thought experiment and see where it leads.

The requirement here, in its simplest form, is that users can post details of their workout, and other users can comment on that – the other points are merely constraints and concessions. If we start here, we may envisage a notice board in each gym where people would perhaps fill out a card such as shown in Figure 4-1.

Workout

Details	
Name	*Ritchie Blackmore*
Length	*2hrs*
Calories	*500*
Comment	*V· Difficult after long break*

***Figure 4-1.** Workout form*

Here, we're asking the user to populate the length of the workout, calories burned, comment, etc. We may then imagine that once this is posted, other users would add Post-it notes to the card. This seems to work well to an extent, but we have a problem with making this scalable: even within the same gym. For example, after a certain number of posts, the board would be full; further, the comments themselves would obstruct the posts.

Let's imagine a slightly different scenario then: a printed sheet of the workouts for that week. After a member has completed their training, they would still fill out a card, but this time, they would hand the card to a member of staff in the gym. The cards would be piled up, and once every day, someone would type them up and print them out. We could follow a similar principle for comments: each time a member wished to comment, they would fill out a card and hand it to a member of staff, who would include the comments in the printout for the following day.

If we wanted to make this work for all the sites then we would, perhaps, have the member of staff post the comments to a central location, who would type out the posts and comments and send the sheets to every gym.

We did say initially that this would not lend itself to a manual process, but I suspect this mental picture will help when thinking about the design of the system.

CQRS

We've already discussed the concept of CQRS when we were looking at event sourcing in Chapter 2. However, in this case, we're examining CQRS in its own right. Let's first remind ourselves of what CQRS is, and then we can explore whether it will help us with our current problem.

CQRS stands for Command Query Responsibility Segregation. According to a 2011 post by Martin Fowler, this was something that was brought into the public domain by Greg Young.

The idea behind this pattern is, as the name suggests, that you segregate parts of your application that read data from those that write it. This provides some huge benefits, but it is far from without cost; we'll explore both here.

Benefits

Let's imagine that we decided to use a typical transactional database for our social media design. Figure 4-2 illustrates a familiar pattern.

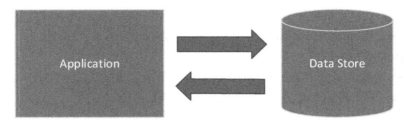

Figure 4-2. *Typical DB access architecture*

The data store in this case is very likely ACID compliant (see Chapter 3). What this means is that each time you write data to a table, the application (and the user) must wait while the data is written, indexes are updated, constraints are checked, etc. This process is lightning fast, and so it can manage a high throughput. At the same time, you're reading information from those same tables and very possibly updating records too. Let's have a look what our relational data structure might look like for our social media solution.

Figure 4-3 shows a potential data structure (in fact, it doesn't really matter what the data structure is for the purposes of this discussion).

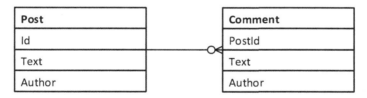

Figure 4-3. *DB table structure*

As posts are being written to the database, comments may be being added. As we've already said, modern databases are incredibly good at performing these types of tasks quickly, but when your user base gets to very big numbers, that might not be quickly *enough*. If that is the case, then we need to ask what we can do about that and what *is* important, and what *is not*.

Since we're listing the benefits of CQRS here, let's think about how using CQRS can help us here. One way it could help is if we created a separate data store and wrote to that instead. To be clear, this need not necessarily be a separate database (although it can be); for example, we could introduce a system such as that shown in Figure 4-4.

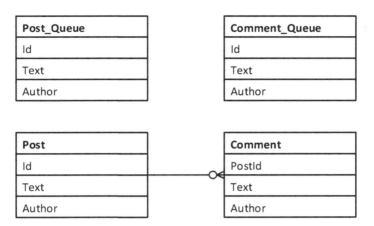

Figure 4-4. *DB structure using CQRS*

You would then have an offline process that simply took the elements of the queue tables and wrote them to the *Post* and *Comment* tables. Although this does provide some benefit, more typically, the *Command* side writes to a different store.

Note   I am very deliberately using the term "data store," rather than database, the reason being that there are many viable places to store such data and they are not all in a typical database.

The principle here is simply that you read from a *read-only* location. The location that you write to is obviously not *write-only*, because you would never be able to extract that information, but effectively you write to a buffer location. It may be that you decide to combine this approach with *event sourcing*; however, you could simply have your write location as a message bus.

As with everything relating to software, this is a trade-off.

Drawbacks

Now that we've seen the benefits of using CQRS, let's talk about the price that you pay. The first and most obvious drawback here is, in fact, the same as the benefit. That is, the benefit is that you have separated read and write functionality, and so you have decoupled perhaps the biggest constraint to scalability; the drawback is that you have separated read and write functionality, and so your data is no longer ***strongly*** consistent; that is, when you read data, you are not guaranteed that you have read the latest version of the data.

Consistency Models

Data consistency refers to the state of the data across the system. For example, if I make a change to the data, a system that is said to be ***strongly consistent*** would show the same data state to all the users of that system; additionally, the user that made that change initially should see that change reflected.

Figure 4-5 illustrates what a strongly consistent system would look like. At a given point in time, all three users shown in Figure 4-5 would need to see the same information when looking for **Field1**.

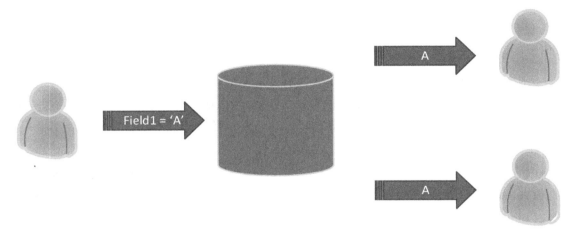

Figure 4-5. *Strongly consistent*

This kind of model is typical when dealing with a system that has a single data store. It is bread and butter for most RDBMSs – a user updates a field, and all other users see that change. However, let's imagine the scenario in Figure 4-6.

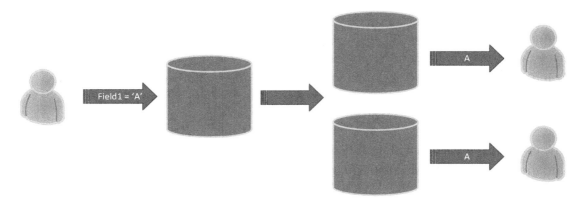

Figure 4-6. *Not strongly consistent*

Looking at Figure 4-6, it's difficult (although not impossible – see the "Distributed Transactions" section in Chapter 3) to imagine a situation where that setup would be strongly consistent.

Note   There are dozens of consistency models. In this section, I'm going to group them into three categories and cover a broad explanation of that category; however, in doing so, we will miss some of the nuance of the individual models.

Strong or Strict Consistency

As we've already alluded to, **strongly consistent** data is data that is reflected across an entire system in such a way that as the data is written, it is visible to all other parts of the system in the order in which it was written.

In this model, we pay a performance price in order the see the same view of the data across the system.

Sequential or Causal Consistency

In ***causal consistency***, we no longer expect to see the data ***as*** it is written across the system; however, we do expect to see the data in the ***order*** in which it was written across the system. For example, if I write three pieces of data, [a, b, c], I would expect to see them written in that order.

In this model, we get better performance than with strong consistency, but we need to maintain the order; this means that an additional payload must travel with the data itself that gives a dependency graph of data. This, therefore, increases the amount of data being passed around and, in order to maintain the order, can result in blocking calls.

Weak or Eventual Consistency

The ***eventual consistency*** model allows a situation where I can write some data and that the data will be available for reading at some stage in the future, but in no guaranteed order.

This is by far the fastest model, but we pay a high price in that you can end up in a situation where either you are unable to see data that has been written or you are able to see it in a state where it is not final; for example, imagine the following customer data:

> *Customer Record: Customer Id, Customer Address Id.*

> *Customer Address Record: Address*

In eventual consistency, we can have a situation where either the address exists without the customer or the customer exists without the address. In fact, the only guarantee that we have is that when we have finished processing (i.e., *eventually*), everything will be created correctly.

For our purposes, eventual consistency seems like an excellent option – if a post is made on the site, it doesn't really matter if that post is not immediately visible, nor does it matter if the comments don't appear at the instant they are posted.

Target Architecture

Our target architecture is going to prefer performance and scalability over immediately consistent data. Let's have a look at our target architecture diagram, and then we can discuss what this looks like in the real world.

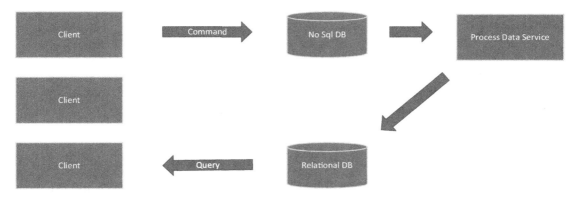

Figure 4-7. *Target architecture*

Looking at the diagram shown in Figure 4-7, we can see that we have a number of clients that both read and write from the data in the system; however, following a write (or a *command* in CQRS parlance), the data is unceremoniously dumped into a NoSQL database. As stated earlier in this chapter, it is not necessary to have a NoSQL database here per se, nor do you need a separate database: CQRS can work within a single database.

Once the data is written to the NoSQL store, a service is responsible for reading what's in that store and writing that to a relational database.

Note   It's no accident that you'll be feeling an overwhelming sense of déjà vu at this stage. Much of what we're describing is very similar to the event sourcing that we discussed in Chapter 2. However, while the implementation details may be similar, the design principle is different; that is, in this chapter, we are separating the read and write access for the purpose of performance, whereas with event sourcing, we separate them out of necessity (i.e., you cannot – or at least *should not* - read from an event stream directly).

You may decide to add a message broker queue as a shock absorber for the service that picks up the data and converts it to relational data. This allows for adjustments to the flow if you find that it takes longer to write the data than to read it; however, in our case, the NoSQL database itself can act as a queue.

Finally, once we have the data in relational form, it can be queried by our client again.

Examples

In our example, we will use a local instance of MongoDB and a local instance of SQL Server. In fact, the architectural principle here requires neither of these specific databases, and so it should be cross applicable; however, while the SQL syntax would broadly work across most relational databases, the NoSQL syntax is specific to the Mongo API (or anything that emulates it, such as Cosmos).

Note   I will continue on the assumption that an instance of SQL Server and an instance of MongoDB are installed locally on your machine. A full explanation of these databases falls beyond the scope of this chapter (and book); however, MongoDB can be found here: www.mongodb.com/, and SQL Server here: www.microsoft.com/en-gb/sql-server/sql-server-downloads.

While we do not need to create a schema for Mongo, we do need to create one for SQL Server.

Schema Creation

Listing 4-1 should create a schema in SQL Server that will work for the purpose of this example.

Listing 4-1. Schema Creation

```
CREATE TABLE [dbo].[Post](
       Text nvarchar(max) NULL,
       WorkoutDate datetime NULL,
       Id uniqueidentifier DEFAULT NEWSEQUENTIALID(),
       PRIMARY KEY (Id)
) ON [PRIMARY] TEXTIMAGE_ON [PRIMARY]
GO

CREATE TABLE [dbo].[Comment](
       [Text] nvarchar(max) NULL,
       PostId uniqueidentifier,
```

```
        Id uniqueidentifier DEFAULT NEWSEQUENTIALID(),
        PRIMARY KEY (Id),
        FOREIGN KEY (PostId) REFERENCES dbo.Post(Id)
) ON [PRIMARY] TEXTIMAGE_ON [PRIMARY]
GO
```

Note   The use of a Sequential GUID has some advantages over using a standard integer to index the table; however, as far as I'm aware, this is a SQL Server–only variable type. Should you decide to use a different RDBMS, just substitute this for an integer.

Looking at our target architecture, there are only two conceptual parts to it (excluding the databases); these are the **Client** and the **Process Data Service**.

Updating the Database

When deciding how we should update the database, there are some architectural decisions to consider.

Update a Local Version of the Database Directly

This approach uses the Mongo instance as a local cache – the instance of Mongo can be installed directly on the client machine, and the client can write to it directly.

As with any architectural decision, security should be considered. The security model here would be that that machine that hosts the website also hosts the MongoDB installation, meaning it would be protected via a firewall; however, at some stage, an application will need to transfer that information to the relational store that we are reading from. This can lead to decisions being made around servers and cloud providers that make this transition easier, cheaper, and safer.

This scenario works well in the case of the client being a website; the server side of the website may write directly to the MongoDB. The advantage here is that you get a much improved write speed; however, you couple your client directly to your database technology.

> **Note**   The archetypal example of why you should abstract access to a database is that you may wish to swap out your database provider. While this is a generally good practice (e.g., for testing), it's very unlikely that you will ever really swap out the database provider.

The approach of having a local instance of Mongo breaks down where, for example, your client is a desktop client. Installing an instance of Mongo in this case would not be feasible in all the locations where your application is installed; this is also true for mobile applications – in which case, this would not only be impractical but also impossible.

> **Note**   While installing Mongo on every client is not feasible, there are other database and caching technologies that would make this possible. In Chapter 6, we discuss just such a scenario.

In our specific case, it seems to make more sense to call a web service to update the database.

Call a Web Service to Update the Database

Calling a web service is an excellent way to provide an abstraction layer on top of your data access, and it also means that you can deal with situations where your client and data are not co-located.

> **Note**   The term "client," in this context, is used to refer to any process or set of processes that consume a service. In our case, the client may be a website; however, the term "client" is overloaded, in that the portion of a website that operates on the user's machine is also "Client."

Because you are securing your web service using some form of token-based authentication, you're less likely to be faced with the same security issues as where you update the MongoDB directly.

Our use case requires that users be able to update this from mobile devices, and so we have little choice but to wrap our update in a web service.

Checking the Data

In the following sections, we are going to write to, and read from, the data. In order to validate that this is happening correctly, we'll need to see the data. There are a number of options; however, for SQL Server, I would recommend downloading **SQL Server Management Studio (SSMS)**, and for Mongo, **MongoDB Compass**.

Listing 4-2. Check Posts and Comments

```
SELECT p.*,
       (SELECT COUNT(1)
       FROM Comment c
       WHERE c.PostId = p.Id) as "Comment Count"
FROM Post p
```

Listing 4-2 gives a SQL script that will display the posts, along with the count of comments next to them. This will be useful later on.

As with previous chapters, all the code can be found in the following GitHub repo:

```
https://github.com/Apress/software-architecture-by-example
```

Web Service

Since we need a web service, our first step is to create one to wrap the database update calls.

Appendix A covers the finer details of creating an API in .Net – so here we'll just list the changes once the API is created (essentially, once the default API project has been created).

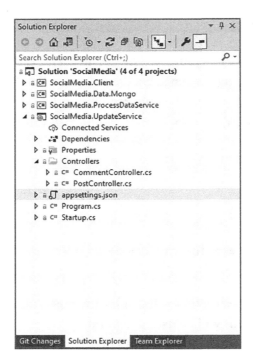

Figure 4-8. *Update service*

As you can see from Figure 4-8, we have two controllers in this project; let's see the
PostController.cs first.

Listing 4-3. PostController.cs

```
[ApiController]
[Route("[controller]")]
public class PostController : ControllerBase
{
    private readonly IMongoDBWrapper _mongoDBWrapper;

    public PostController(IMongoDBWrapper mongoDBWrapper)
    {
        _mongoDBWrapper = mongoDBWrapper;
    }
```

```
[HttpPost]
public async Task<string> Create() =>
    await _mongoDBWrapper.CreatePost(DateTime.Now, $"test post
    {DateTime.Now}");
}
```

There's very little to this class, as you can see. However, we are utilizing a wrapper class (**MongoDBWrapper**), which provides the method **CreatePost**. We'll come to that helper project soon, but first, let's see the code in Listing 4-4 for the comment update.

Listing 4-4. CommentController.cs

```
[ApiController]
[Route("[controller]")]
public class CommentController : ControllerBase
{
    private readonly IMongoDBWrapper _mongoDBWrapper;

    public CommentController(IMongoDBWrapper mongoDBWrapper)
    {
        _mongoDBWrapper = mongoDBWrapper;
    }

    [HttpPost]
    public async Task Create(string postId) =>
        await _mongoDBWrapper.CreateComment($"test comment {DateTime.
        Now}", postId);

}
```

Before we discuss the wrapper itself, let's see how that is registered in the Asp.Net DI container (Listing 4-5).

Listing 4-5. Startup.cs

```
public void ConfigureServices(IServiceCollection services)
{
    services.AddControllers();
    services.AddSwaggerGen(c =>
    {
        c.SwaggerDoc("v1", new OpenApiInfo { Title = "SocialMedia.
        UpdateService", Version = "v1" });
    });

    services.AddSingleton<IMongoDBWrapper, MongoDBWrapper>();
}
```

Let's now discuss how we might access the MongoDB to update it – spoiler: this will essentially be filling in the methods that we've used before.

Accessing MongoDB

In order to access the MongoDB, we're going to create a wrapper project.

Note   A ***wrapper*** or ***proxy*** project or class is simply a way to insulate yourself from a third party. The idea is that your code calls the wrapper, and the wrapper, in turn, calls the third party. This gives you a number of advantages: should the third-party make a breaking change to some method, then you have only a single place to change that interaction; further, you can control the abstraction within your own project for the purpose of testing; and finally, you have a single place to log and debug issues with the third-party interaction.

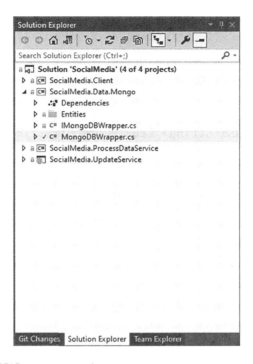

Figure 4-9. *MongoDBWrapper project*

As you will see from Figure 4-9, we have a very simple project, consisting of an interface and implementation class.

Note   As you'll see from the code, the location of the MongoDB and the database name are hard-coded – this is done partly to simplify the example, but also for readability. Such values should not be stored in the code.

Listing 4-6 shows the **CreateComment** and **CreatePost** methods.

Listing 4-6. MongoDBWrapper.cs

```
public class MongoDBWrapper : IMongoDBWrapper
{
    readonly IMongoDatabase _db;
```

```
public MongoDBWrapper()
{
    var dbClient = new MongoClient("mongodb://localhost:27017");
    _db = dbClient.GetDatabase("SocialMedia");
}

public async Task<string> CreateComment(string comment,
string postId)
{
    var newComment = new Comment()
    {
        PostId = postId,
        Text = comment
    };

    var collection = _db.GetCollection<Comment>("Comments");
    await collection.InsertOneAsync(newComment);

    return newComment.Id.ToString();
}

public async Task<string> CreatePost(DateTime workoutDate, string
comment)
{
    var newPost = new Post()
    {
        WorkoutDate = workoutDate,
        Text = comment
    };

    var collection = _db.GetCollection<Post>("Posts");
    await collection.InsertOneAsync(newPost);

    return newPost.Id.ToString();
}
```

I've listed these two methods together in Listing 4-6, as they, essentially, do the same thing – firstly, they instantiate an object (e.g., **Comment** or **Post**) with appropriate values. Following this, we get a typed collection from Mongo; that is, we ask the DB for a collection of Posts or Comments; and then, once we have one, we add to that collection and return the ID.

We also need methods to return the next **Post** and the next **Comment**. Listing 4-7 shows these methods.

Listing 4-7. MongoDBWrapper.cs

```
public async Task<Post> GetNextPost()
{
    var collection = _db.GetCollection<Post>("Posts");
    var result = await collection.FindOneAndDeleteAsync(a => true);
    return result;
}

public async Task<Comment> GetNextComment(string postId)
{
    var collection = _db.GetCollection<Comment>("Comments");
    var result = await collection.FindOneAndDeleteAsync(a =>
    a.PostId == postId);
    return result;
}
```

In Listing 4-7, we can see that we first return the collection as before using the **GetCollection** method; then, instead of inserting, we call **FindOneAndDeleteAsync**; this takes the first record that it finds according to the criteria provided, returns the record, and then deletes it (so that we don't re-read the record).

Note   There are, essentially, two ways that you can process data in this way, and they both have advantages and disadvantages. The way that we're using here reads and deletes the record and then writes that record to another location; the downside here is that if the system crashes between the two processes, the record may be lost. The alternative is to read the record, then write that to the destination system, and then delete it from the source; this has the advantage that no data is lost, but the downside is that it is slower – in some cases, much slower.

The next thing that we'll need to do is to create our client application.

The Client

The client application, for this example, will simply be a console application. We're basically going to call the web services – as we discussed earlier, given the required deployment model, we have little choice on this.

Listing 4-8 shows the menu of the application.

Listing 4-8. Program.cs

```
static async Task Main(string[] args)
{
    while (true)
    {
        Console.WriteLine("Choose action");
        Console.WriteLine("1: Create Post");
        Console.WriteLine("2: Comment on Post");
        Console.WriteLine("3: Create Post and Comment");
        Console.WriteLine("4: Small Bulk Test");
        Console.WriteLine("5: Large Bulk Test");

        Console.WriteLine("0: Exit");

        var result = Console.ReadKey();
        switch (result.Key)
        {
            case ConsoleKey.D1:
                await CreatePost();
                break;

            case ConsoleKey.D2:
                await CreateComment();
                break;

            case ConsoleKey.D3:
                var postId = await CreateSinglePost();
                await CreateComment(postId);
                break;
```

```
        case ConsoleKey.D4:
            for (int i = 1; i <= 100; i++)
            {
                await CreatePost();
                await CreateComment();
            }
            break;

        case ConsoleKey.D5:
            for (int i = 1; i <= 100; i++)
            {
                Console.WriteLine($"Processing batch {i}");
                for (int j = 1; j <= 100; j++)
                {
                    await CreatePost();
                    await CreateComment();
                }
                await Task.Delay(20);
            }
            break;

        case ConsoleKey.D0:
            return;
        }
    }
}
```

There's quite a lot of code here, but it's all very simple: we display the menu and then respond to the keypress. Options 1 and 2 create a single **Post** or **Comment;** option 3 creates a **Post** and then a **Comment** for that **Post**; options 4 and 5 are for the purpose of testing load, and they create many posts and comments.

In Listing 4-9, we can see the **CreateSinglePost** method.

Listing 4-9. Program.cs

```
private static async Task<string> CreateSinglePost()
{
    var httpClient = HttpClientFactory.Create();

    var httpContent = new StringContent("");
    var result = await httpClient.PostAsync("https://
    localhost:44388/Post", httpContent);

    Debug.Assert(result.IsSuccessStatusCode);

    return result.Content.ToString();
}
```

The first thing we do here is use the **HttpClientFactory** to create an **HttpClient** object. The **HttpClient** object allows us to make HTTP calls outside of the application.

Note   The **HttpClientFactory** provides several advantages over instantiating an **HttpClient** directly; however, the most important is that it prevents *socket exhaustion*: the issue here being that as an **HttpClient** is disposed of, it takes some additional time for the underlying socket to be released; using a factory pattern means that the same instance of the HttpClient can be reused.

Following this, we call **PostAsync** to invoke the **HttpPost** method of the controller.

Note   You may notice a **Debug.Assert( )** call. This is a mechanism to ensure that during development, certain things are true about your code; where they are not, the code will break (essentially, this functions as a conditional breakpoint).

The **CreateComment** is a virtually identical method, as you will see from Listing 4-10.

Listing 4-10. Program.cs

```
private static async Task CreateComment(string postId = null)
{
    if (postId == null) postId = _posts.GetRandom();

    var httpClient = HttpClientFactory.Create();

    var httpContent = new StringContent(postId);
    var result = await httpClient.PostAsync("https://localhost:44388/
    Comment", httpContent);

    Debug.Assert(result.IsSuccessStatusCode);
}
```

From the code in Listing 4-10, we can see that the only real difference is that the **CreateComment** method accepts a parameter, which it passes to the /**comment** endpoint. Also, **CreateComment** does not return a value, whereas **CreateSinglePost** does; you'll notice that we're accepting this parameter as optional and, where it isn't supplied, we pick a random **Post**.

Note   The idea behind picking a random post is for testing purposes only. Clearly, if this were a real system, each comment would be attached to whichever post it was made about.

The only part of this code that's now missing is the **CreatePost** method, which we can see along with a class level static variable in Listing 4-11.

Listing 4-11. Program.cs

```
    static readonly List<string> _posts = new List<string>();

    private static async Task CreatePost()
    {
        var createPostResult = await CreateSinglePost();
        _posts.Add(createPostResult);
    }
```

Listing 4-11 shows that when a post is created, we add that post to an in-memory list of posts.

The final piece of the puzzle is the offline process that reads from the MongoDB and writes that information to SQL Server.

Process Data Service

The **ProcessDataService** is a very simple console application.

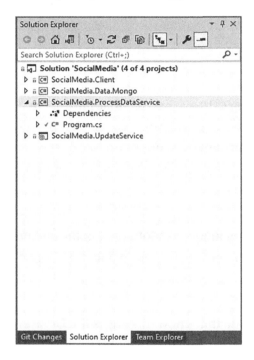

Figure 4-10. *ProcessDataService*

As Figure 4-10 illustrates, the **ProcessDataService** has a single code file. In fact, it consists of only three methods; Listing 4-12 shows the Main method.

Listing 4-12. Program.cs

```
static async Task Main(string[] args)
{
    using var connection = new SqlConnection(@"Data Source=.\
    SQLEXPRESS;Initial Catalog=SocialMedia;Integrated
    Security=True;");
    connection.Open();

    await ReadPosts(connection, new MongoDBWrapper());
}
```

As we can see, all we're doing here is establishing a SQL Server connection, an instance of the **MongoDBWrapper**, and passing both into a separate method: **ReadPosts**.

Listing 4-13 shows the ReadPosts method.

Listing 4-13. Program.cs

```
private static async Task ReadPosts(SqlConnection connection,
MongoDBWrapper wrapper)
{
    while (true)
    {
        // Read from Mongo
        var nextPost = await wrapper.GetNextPost();
        if (nextPost == null) break;

        Console.WriteLine($"ReadPosts: Read {nextPost.Id}");

        using var transaction = connection.BeginTransaction();

        // Write To Sql Server
        string sql = "DECLARE @newRecord table(newId uniqueidentifier); "
                        + "INSERT INTO Post "
                        + "(Text, WorkoutDate) "
                        + "OUTPUT INSERTED.Id INTO @newRecord "
```

```
                              + "VALUES "
                              + "(@text, @workoutDate) "
                              + "SELECT CONVERT(nvarchar(50), newId) FROM @
                              newRecord";
        var result = await connection.QueryAsync<string>(sql,
                    new { text = nextPost.Text, workoutDate = nextPost.
                    WorkoutDate },
                    transaction);

        // Get all comments for post
        await ReadComments(transaction, connection,
                    result.Single(), nextPost.Id.ToString(), wrapper);

        transaction.Commit();
    }

    Console.WriteLine("ReadPosts: End");
}
```

In Listing 4-13, we can see that the **ReadPosts** method is a loop that is exited only where **GetNextPost** returns null; that is, where there are no further posts available. Following this, a transaction is established (for more discussion on transactions, please see Chapter 3). We then insert the post into the SQL table and subsequently call ReadComments (see Listing 4-14). Following this, we commit the transaction.

Note   It's worth noting that, as we stated earlier, should the transaction fail and the code crash, the post that was read from the Mongo database would be lost; in our situation, we've made the decision that we can live with such data loss; however, many systems cannot live with data loss of any kind.

Listing 4-14. Program.cs

```
private static async Task ReadComments(SqlTransaction transaction,
SqlConnection connection,
    string postId, string filterPostId, IMongoDBWrapper wrapper)
{
```

```
while (true)
{
    // Read from Mongo
    var nextComment = await wrapper.
    GetNextComment(filterPostId);
    if (nextComment == null) break;

    // Write To Sql Server
    string sql = "INSERT INTO Comment "
                + "(Text, PostId) "
                + "VALUES "
                + "(@text, @postId)";

    var result = await connection.ExecuteAsync(sql,
        new { text = nextComment.Text, postId = postId },
        transaction);
}
}
```

The **ReadComments** in Listing 4-14 method is very similar to the **ReadPosts** method
that we saw earlier; we read the comments from the Mongo database and try to insert
them into the relational database; we do this using the same transaction, meaning that
the post and comments will either get written together or not at all.

Note   As we've said, transactions are covered in more detail in Chapter 3;
however, transactions, or at least transactions that span several operations, are
not always an entirely good thing. It may be that if there were a system error,
having the **Post** without the **Comment** may have value; it would certainly improve
throughput to dispense of this transaction.

Figure 4-11 shows the data that has been transferred from the MongoDB across to
the relational database.

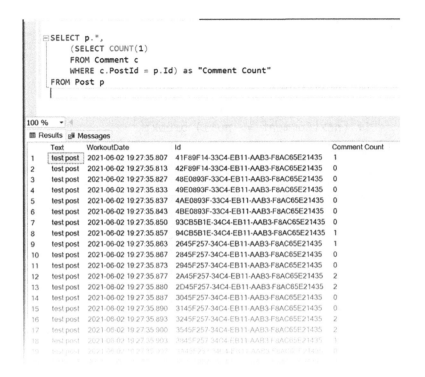

Figure 4-11. SQL Server data

Summary

We have focused heavily in this chapter on scalability, and we've paid a hefty price for it. The kind of scale that we're talking about here is far beyond what an average system will need to deal with – in many cases, a CQRS system such as this would be overkill and simply add complexity. However, if used at the right time, it can help you to scale your system: especially when immediate consistency is not a restricting factor.

In this chapter, we've also covered using a NoSQL database as a kind of dump. This is another view on using CQRS, which is that you can allow the customer to leave the point of interaction (sale, purchase, or whatever) and just keep the raw transaction to process later. You can then do whatever you choose with that data at a later time. This particular facet is concerned more with performance (or at least perceived performance) than scalability – although it does relate to both.

If we return to our, by now familiar, trick of imagining a sale (for example) in a real-world scenario, writing a transaction to a SQL relational database would be akin to getting out a general ledger in front of the customer and entering their transaction in it, reconciling the VAT, and other accounts. Obviously, computers do these things quickly, so you may be able to do such things while they wait, but if you find that the checkout process is taking seconds, rather than milliseconds, then maybe it's time to reconsider exactly what you're asking the customer to wait for.

CHAPTER 5

The Admin Application Problem

One of the biggest problems that software engineers and architects face during their day-to-day work is deciding when something is *done*. In the past, I've worked on both large and small-scale software systems that we would produce and then sell on to customers; but the questions that we'd get from customers, be they internal or external, were always of the same vein: "Can you just add x?" or "Can we change y?" Often, it's cost prohibitive as a software vendor to make minor changes for individual customers; imagine a situation where you could contact Microsoft and ask them to change the icon of Microsoft Word!

Microsoft and many other companies have established a system around this, which is to make the software configurable and extensible. You can, for example, create add-ins for the Office suite.

In this chapter, we'll explore ways that we can extend a piece of software without changing the core components of that software.

© Paul Michaels 2022
P. Michaels, *Software Architecture by Example*, https://doi.org/10.1007/978-1-4842-7990-8_5

Background

The software company that you are working for produces CRM (Customer Relationship Management) software. Several of your customers that use the software have requested an administration program that allows them to update their customer records. However, each of the customers needs the software to operate in a slightly different manner.

Note   Clearly, the CRM system that your company produces is in its infancy, as it is yet to produce something that maintains the customer records.

Let's define the scope of this task.

Requirements

The MVP, or Minimum Viable Product, for this application is that the system will:

- Read or create a JSON data file, which will define a customer, including name, address, email, and credit limit.

- Allow the creation of new customer records.

- Allow the user to change existing records.

This constitutes the functionality that all of the customers have requested; however, three have requested additional, specific functionality:

- Ability to email the customer when the record has changed.

- Ability to display an alert on the screen where the credit limit is set to more than £300.

- Ability to list any customers over a given credit limit.

Let's think about how we can achieve this and produce the software that best meets the needs of all the customers.

Options

In previous chapters, we've discussed how we might achieve our goal using a manual process; this chapter will be no different, but in this instance, the requirement is to maintain a record that is stored on a computer.

Manual Process

The reason it's useful to consider the manual process is that it starkly reveals exactly what the requirements are. In this instance, the requirement is to maintain a file that's stored on a server (the JSON data file).

If we imagine a manual process for this, we might think about an IT administrator, whose job is to manually alter this file. To give us a feel for the type of work involved, Listing 5-1 shows an example of the file itself.

Listing 5-1. Customer Data File

```
{
  "Customers": [
    {
      "Name": "Fred Bains",
      "Address": "1 Hilltop View, Swansea",
      "Email": "fred@bains125.com",
      "CreditLimit": 100
    },
    {
      "Name": "Wilma Green",
      "Address": "84 Elm Close, Luton",
      "Email": "wilma.ann.green@thegreens.com",
      "CreditLimit": 400
    }
  ]
}
```

Each of our customers has their own data file, so there is no risk that one customer could access a different customer's data.

Note   Unfortunately, the term "customer" is overloaded here. The one type of customer is the customer that has purchased your software, and the other type is the customer that *they have* for *their* business.

We can imagine a manual process whereby somebody may go and change this file; in fact, JSON is a very human-readable format, so it wouldn't take a huge amount of training. For the additional requirements, we can certainly see how a user might be able to email an alert; however, producing reports based on a JSON file is a little different and may be difficult to do manually. It seems like an obvious thing, but we state that, given the manual process, the varying requirements become irrelevant, as each customer would simply implement their own additional requirements.

Each of these operators would be given a runbook of sorts, for example:

Amend Customer

1. Open the JSON data file in Notepad.

2. Find the relevant customer by searching for their name.

3. Change the record.

4. Email the customer using the email address on the record explaining that their record has been updated.

Now, let's consider what this might look like for a different operator:

Amend Customer

1. Open the JSON data file in Notepad.

2. Find the relevant customer by searching for their name.

3. Change the record.

4. Check the credit limit – if it is greater than £300, then notify the person that requested the change.

As we can see, the two processes are identical except for the last step.

Essentially, what we are looking for is a method that we can encapsulate this manual change in a software system. We can imagine that one such way might be to change the source code for each different implementation; a pseudocode version of this idea might look like Listing 5-2.

Listing 5-2. Pseudocode Implementation of Differing Requirements by Customer

```
UpdateRecord()
If Customer = "Customer1" Then
        If CreditLimit > 300 Then
                SendAlert()
Else If Customer = "Customer2" Then
        SendNotification();
End If
```

In fact, I've personally seen variations of Listing 5-2 being used to satisfy the requirements of multiple clients. Even apart from other concerns, it becomes increasingly difficult to maintain code like this: the complexity increasing almost exponentially as new customers are added (imagine if *Customer 4* wanted alerting and notifications).

Situations like this led to the *Open-Closed Principle*; this forms part of the SOLID design principles; it seems strange that we've reached Chapter 5 of a book on software architecture and have yet to speak about the SOLID design principles, so we'll correct that now!

SOLID

SOLID is, in fact, an acronym; most of these principles can be attributed to Robert Martin, Bertrand Meyer, and Barbara Liskov; in brief, they are:

1. Single Responsibility.

2. Open-Closed.

3. Liskov Substitution.

4. Interface Segregation.

5. Dependency Inversion.

Although we are currently interested in the Open-Closed Principle, let's briefly describe all of these principles – while I don't necessarily think that software that follows all of these principles becomes *good* software, they are doubtless good principles to be aware of.

Single Responsibility

A class should have only one reason to change.

The Single Responsibility Principle dictates that there should only be a single reason to change a piece of code. As with all these principles, the best description of what this means is to state what it is trying to guard against.

Let's consider a class that might exist in our software: the **Customer** class. Now, let's imagine that the Customer class looks like Listing 5-3.

Listing 5-3. A Possible Customer Class

```
public class Customer
{
    public string Name { get; set; }
    public string UpdateNameInDatabase(string newName)
    {
        ...
    }
    public bool SendEmailNotification(string emailBody)
    {
        ...
    }
}
```

The class in Listing 5-3 would violate the Single Responsibility Principle (SRP) because it would have more than one reason to change; that is, it does more than one thing.

Let's imagine that we want to change our class, such that the formatting of the name changes to always be uppercase when we read it – so a change to the in-memory representation of the data is *one reason* for the class to change. What if we updated the structure of the database, such that the customer name has now two fields? We would need to change the in-memory representation and the **UpdateNameInDatabase** method. Now, what if we wanted to add attachments to our email notification? Again, our class would need to change for a *second reason*.

As we can see, our class does not follow the Single Responsibility Principle very well at all!

However, the principles in the SOLID acronym are not some kind of litany that we should simply remember and follow without question; in fact, all software engineering principles should be continually questioned. What is wrong with having to change the class for multiple reasons?

Well, there are a few issues here; let's focus on the following three: testability, code churn, and the resilience of the software in general.

Testability

Ultimately, all software is testable and tested – unless you simply write it and then instantly delete it, it will be both tested and testable. How can we ensure that our class correctly writes the customer name to the database? Well, one option is that we have faith that the functionality works, and we deploy this to our customer base. Does this mean that the software is neither tested nor testable? On the contrary: the software will be tested by our customer base, and it will be tested by using the functionality that we state is available.

I won't say here that such a method is flawed (your customers may do so if you adopt this approach), although I will offer an alternative: that we create a unit test against our method; the issue here is that our method writes to the database, and so we would need to abstract that part of the functionality; however, we can't do that because our class has both the business logic and the database access built in.

Code Churn

Changing code is dangerous. To clarify exactly what I mean by that statement: there is a non-zero risk that for every line of code you write or change, you will introduce an unexpected bug or change the behavior in an unexpected manner. Computer programs are extremely complex, and computer programmers are fallible, so each time code changes, there's a chance that something will go wrong. In my time as a programmer, I have seen the most innocuous changes result in hugely significant bugs.

Obviously, changing the code of a program that is currently broken inherently carries less risk than changing the code of a program that is working well. However, if we accept that code churn (i.e., the act of changing code) is dangerous (relative to not changing the code), then anything we can do to isolate, insulate, and reduce change must, therefore, be a good thing.

If a class does more than one thing, there is more than one *reason to change* it, which means that it is more likely to *need to change* and therefore is more likely to break.

Software Resilience

Addressing this separately from the other two reasons, let's look at the resilience of the software at rest; by that, I mean the chances that a piece of code has a bug that has yet to be detected. As we've already said, software is complex; bugs can be present in software for years and years before coming to light. Let's imagine a situation where the tool that we're using to send emails fails for some reason; well, in our example here, that failure could affect our entire class, meaning that we are unable to update or retrieve customer information, simply because we are unable to send emails.

A Better Way

As I've said multiple times throughout this book, there are no **right** or **wrong** decisions in software, and these rules are no exception; adhering to these rules has a cost. However, let's imagine our class slightly differently and think about what the differences may cost.

Listing 5-4. A Better Way?

```
public class Customer
{
    public string Name { get; set; }
}

public class CustomerRepository
{
    public UpdateName(Customer customer)
    {
        ...
    }
}

public class EmailService
{
    public bool Send(string emailBody, string to)
    {
        ...
    }
}
```

In Listing 5-4, we have separated our single class into three. We have a class that is responsible for updating the database, we have a class that is responsible for sending emails (which incidentally had no dependency on the **Customer** at all now), and the **Customer** class itself only represents the in-memory state of the customer.

As we've said, there's no free lunch here; we've solved the problems expressed, but we've introduced an element of complexity. In the example that we have here, the complexity that we've introduced actually simplifies the implementation; however, this is not always the case; as with everything in software design, you should declare the benefits that you intend to get out of something and then weigh that against the cost. If this system was working as Listing 5-3 for years and had never changed or had an issue, then you should consider what benefits you'll get from changing it; if the system is constantly breaking and needing to be changed, then you may find it warrants the time and cost to make the change.

The next in the list is the **Open-Closed Principle**; since this is the particular principle that we're interested, we'll delve a little deeper into this one.

Open-Closed

A module will be said to be open if it is still available for extension. For example, it should be possible to add fields to the data structures it contains, or new elements to the set of functions it performs.

A module will be said to be closed if it is available for use by other modules. This assumes that the module has been given a well-defined, stable description (the interface in the sense of information hiding).

The **Open-Closed Principle** is, perhaps, one of the more esoteric of the principles, but at its heart, it's actually quite simple. The idea is that it should be possible to modify the *behavior* of the software without changing the *code* for that software.

Talking specifically about object-oriented programming (for which the principle was initially stated), we essentially have two approaches here: inheritance and polymorphism. In this section, we'll discuss the particular meaning of the Open-Closed Principle, and then we'll also step back and look at what that might mean in a modern software development scenario.

Note   Arguably, in certain cases, using inheritance may be considered polymorphic; however, I think the two approaches here are distinct.

Inheritance

Let's start with inheritance and consider a class as defined in Listing 5-5.

Listing 5-5. EmailService

```
public class EmailService
{
    public virtual bool Send(string emailBody, string to)
    {
        Console.WriteLine("Email Sent");
        return false;
    }
}
```

What we're trying to do is to add functionality to the **Send** method without changing the code. In fact, using inheritance makes this an easy task, as we can see in Listing 5-6.

Listing 5-6. LoggerEmailService

```
    public class LoggerEmailService : EmailService
    {
        public override bool Send(string emailBody, string to)
        {
            var result = base.Send(emailBody, to);

            Console.WriteLine($"Logger: {emailBody}");

            return result;
        }
    }
```

As we can see, the functionality of the method has been extended, and yet the original code remains intact. There are downsides to using the approach; for example, the code that calls this method may initially refer to the **EmailService** and would now need to refer to the new **LoggerEmailService**. We can simply replace any instance of **EmailService** with its subclass, but we are now changing code (albeit fewer lines).

We'll come back to inheritance when we get to the **Liskov Substitution Principle**, as using inheritance can lead to some potential issues.

Perhaps, then, a better way is polymorphism.

Polymorphism

Typically, the polymorphic approach makes use of an interface. Our class from Listing 5-5 may be changed to implement an interface, as shown in Listing 5-7.

Listing 5-7. LoggerEmailService with Interface

```
public class EmailService : IEmailService
{
    public virtual bool Send(string emailBody, string to)
    {
        Console.WriteLine("Email Sent");
        return false;
    }
}
```

The idea behind the approach taken in Listing 5-7 is that any code that references **EmailService** would actually reference **IEmailService** as an abstraction. This means that we can replace the instance of **IEmailService** with any implementation that we choose to use at a given time.

The interface is a contract; it provides no functionality of its own, but anything that implements an interface commits to provide functionality for each of its methods; or, at least commits to *implement* each of the methods; you are free to implement an interface method that does nothing; we'll come back to this shortly.

Note   In C#, since version 8, there has been a concept of *Default Implementations*; this allows the provision of some functionality within an interface. This also blurs the line between the concepts of inheritance and polymorphism further.

Given that we've already established that we can replace a class with its subclass, what advantages does the use of an interface abstraction give us?

Well, the advantage to this approach is that the interface can be replaced with any functionality you choose; for example, and very commonly, you may wish to swap out the interface for an implementation that does nothing at all – for the purpose of testing. Many languages and frameworks (C# and .Net included) have a concept of mocking libraries; these do just that, and provide you with an implementation of an interface that does nothing.

We've mentioned the **Liskov Substitution Principle** already in this section; let's now explore exactly what that is.

Liskov Substitution

Let Φ(x) be a property provable about objects x of type T. Then Φ(y) should be true for objects y of type S where S is a subtype of T.

Despite this mouthful, this is a straightforward idea. The Liskov Substitution Principle (LSP) essentially says that for any class that uses inheritance, the parent class must be replaceable by the subclass. For some reason that I can't fathom, every single example ever used for this is with squares and rectangles.

For our example, let's return to Listing 5-5; in this, we have an **EmailService** class; we don't really have an implementation, but we can imagine that this sends an email. However, what if we wanted to send an SMS; we could do something like Listing 5-8.

Listing 5-8. SMSService

```
public class SMSService : EmailService
{
    public override bool Send(string emailBody, string to)
    {
        //return base.Send(emailBody, to);
        Console.WriteLine("Sent SMS");
        return false;
    }
}
```

The example given in Listing 5-8 is extreme; you probably don't need to understand the LSP to see that this is a poor design (and a little pointless), but what about something slightly more nuanced. Let's consider Listing 5-9.

Listing 5-9. EmailServiceExtended

```
public class EmailServiceExtended : EmailService
{
    public override bool Send(string emailBody, string to)
    {
        //return base.Send(emailBody, to);
        throw new Exception("This method is deprecated");
    }

    public bool Send(string emailBody, string[] to)
    {
        foreach (var destination in to)
        {
            if (!base.Send(emailBody, destination)) return false;
        }

        return true;
    }
}
```

In Listing 5-9, we are extending the functionality of the class. It's easy to imagine a situation where you only want to replace this one method in a huge class with hundreds of lines of code; however, this clearly violates the LSP. It does so because we cannot exchange the base class for the subclass – the code would start to crash.

From this, we can see that there are situations, then, where an interface may make more sense. The next principle, **Interface Segregation Principle**, deals with how interfaces should be partitioned.

Interface Segregation Principle

No client should be forced to depend on methods it does not use.

The idea behind the **Interface Segregation Principle** is a very simple one: don't have a client implement an interface with methods that it doesn't use. For an example, let's look back at Listing 5-7; here, we implement an interface with a single method, which we are using. We could, at this point, imagine an interface that included both email and SMS methods, and a class each which had to stub out or throw exceptions for invalid use; however, we won't because such an interface is very obviously too broad (and would breach other principles that we've mentioned).

Let's instead imagine a very slightly larger interface, such as that in Listing 5-10.

Listing 5-10. IEmailService with Receive

```
public interface IEmailService
{
    bool Send(string emailBody, string to);
    string Receive();
}
```

Listing 5-10 looks innocuous; after all, you might imagine that in addition to sending an email, we would want to receive one too. That may, indeed, be the case and, if you can guarantee that it is always the case, you will not fall foul of the ISP; however, Listing 5-11 shows how this kind of interface can quickly lead to problems.

Listing 5-11. EmailSendService with Receive

```
public class EmailSendService : IEmailService
{
    public string Receive()
    {
        throw new NotImplementedException();
    }

    public virtual bool Send(string emailBody, string to)
    {
        Console.WriteLine("Email Sent");
        return false;
    }
}
```

Here, we have tried to create a granular class (i.e., to adhere to the SRP), and yet we have fallen foul of the ISP because our interface is too broad. Most languages, including C#, allow the implementation of multiple interfaces, so keeping interfaces small makes more sense.

Finally, let's look at the **Dependency Inversion Principle**.

Dependency Inversion Principle

High-level modules should not depend on low-level modules. Both should depend on abstractions (e.g., interfaces).

Abstractions should not depend on details. Details (concrete implementations) should depend on abstractions.

The Dependency Inversion Principle (DIP) rounds off the list – the wording of all of these principles is, sadly, overly complex for what they are trying to convey. In fact, this principle is why IoC containers have become so popular; certainly in the .Net community and in the wider software development community.

In order to understand this principle, let's take Listing 5-12, which shows a piece of code that uses our **EmailService** from Listing 5-7.

Listing 5-12. Program Using EmailService

```
class Program
{
    static void Test()
    {
        var emailService = new EmailService();
        emailService.Send("This is a test email", "great.
        scott.88@1985.com");
    }
}
```

The DIP states that high-level modules (i.e., our program) should not **depend** on low-level modules (i.e., our service), but that both should depend on abstractions. The code in Listing 5-12 breaks this rule because we have a direct dependency. If you were to delete the **EmailService**, the program would not only stop running, it wouldn't even compile.

Surely, though, we need to use the **EmailService** within our program; if we can't use it, then we might as well never create it. The solution is to be found in the second part of the statement: *Both should depend on abstractions.* Listing 5-13 offers a slightly different version of the code in Listing 5-12 but replaces the dependency with an abstraction.

Listing 5-13. Program Using IEmailService

```
class Program
{
    static void Test(IEmailService emailService)
    {
        emailService.Send("This is a test email", "great.
        scott.88@1985.com");
    }
}
```

The idea posited in Listing 5-13 is called **Dependency Injection**, and it comes directly from this principle: we are now passing in an interface, rather than the class itself; this means that we can now delete **EmailService** and the code will still compile; of course, we are required to provide something that fulfills the contract of **IEmailService**, but we no longer directly depend on that particular service. This doesn't completely **invert the dependency**: rather than the program being dependent on the service, we are passing the dependency in.

Inversion of Control

One technique that has become very popular in recent years for enforcing the DIP is the use of an **Inversion of Control** (IoC) container. The idea here is that you register your dependencies with the container, which is then responsible for the lifetime and resolution of those dependencies. Several frameworks, including ASP.NET Core and ASP.NET 5+, have this feature built in. In this scenario, you delegate the dependency injection that we just saw to a separate component; this solves a number of problems, although you still cannot get away from the fact that you must provide an implementation for the abstraction.

Methods of Extending Software

In our manual process, we had a core set of functionality (a set of instructions that everyone followed), but then we had an extension point – that is, parts where the functionality would diverge dependent on the user or situation. This is exactly what we can do with our architecture; essentially, the main ways that we can achieve this are through hooks, messages, and injection.

Hooks

A hook is a point in the program where you call a function or method, but that function or method is replaceable. Let's try to envision this in a tangible, real-world, example.

You have a friend that you send a mail to every year and ask which present their mother would like for Christmas; your friend receives the mail and then replies with their choice, presumably after undertaking some form of research or procedure to discover the answer.

Figure 5-1 illustrates the process described. The hook is a hook because your friend is able to do absolutely anything they wish at this point: They may ask their mother, they may conduct a machine learning experiment, they may place an advert in the local paper asking what the reader's opinions are, or they may do nothing and simply reply with "A box of chocolates."

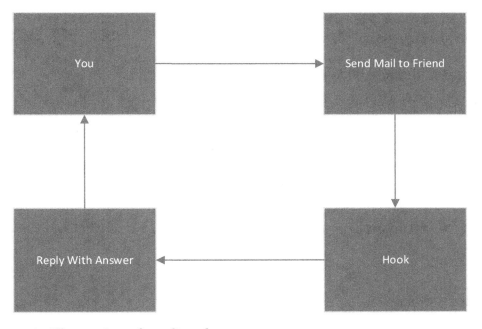

Figure 5-1. *Illustration of sending the message*

In practical terms, a hook can be an event, allowing the user to *hook* into the code flow.

Messages

We have visited this idea in previous chapters. As we saw, we can use a message broker to call out and accept information back into the system. Further, we can achieve a similar effect inside the process by the use of the Mediator Pattern.

Mediator

The Mediator Pattern was featured in the famous Gang of Four book *Design Patterns: Elements of Reusable Object-Oriented Software* and works very well to provide a type of internal message bus.

At its core, the Mediator Pattern can be thought of in the following manner: imagine that we have an **EmailService** class and an **SMSService** class, and then imagine that we wish to communicate between the two (as per Listing 5-14) – we would need to pick a direction of communication (i.e., one of these must be the instigator of the other, or else we would need to pass a reference of each into the other).

Listing 5-14. EmailService and SMSService

```
class EmailService
{
    public bool Send(string emailBody, string to)
    {
        Console.WriteLine("Email Sent");
        // Notify SMS
        return true;
    }
}

class SMSService
{
    public bool Send(string msgBody, string to)
    {
        Console.WriteLine("SMS Sent");
        // Notify Email
        return true;
    }
}
```

At it's very simplest, the Mediator Pattern allows an abstraction over the communication – essentially a linking class – as shown in Listing 5-15. In principle, all we're actually doing here is passing a single instance of a class into both of the instantiated classes (**EmailService** and **SMSService**) and then allowing that class to reference and communicate back with them.

Listing 5-15. Using CommsMediator

```
interface IMessageReceiver
{
    void ReceiveMessage(string message);
}

class CommsMediator
{
    public List<IMessageReceiver> MessageReceivers = new
    List<IMessageReceiver>();

    public void SendMessage(string message)
    {
        foreach (var receiver in MessageReceivers)
        {
            receiver.ReceiveMessage(message);
        }
    }
}

class EmailService : IMessageReceiver
{
    private readonly CommsMediator _commsMediator;

    public EmailService(CommsMediator commsMediator)
    {
        _commsMediator = commsMediator;
    }
```

```
        public void ReceiveMessage(string message)
        {
            Console.WriteLine(message);
        }

        public bool Send(string emailBody, string to)
        {
            Console.WriteLine("Email Sent");
            // Notify SMS
            _commsMediator.SendMessage("email sent");

            return true;
        }
    }

    class SMSService : IMessageReceiver
    {
        private readonly CommsMediator _commsMediator;

        public SMSService(CommsMediator commsMediator)
        {
            _commsMediator = commsMediator;
        }

        public void ReceiveMessage(string message)
        {
            Console.WriteLine(message);
        }

        public bool Send(string msgBody, string to)
        {
            Console.WriteLine("SMS Sent");
            // Notify Email
            _commsMediator.SendMessage("sms sent");

            return true;
        }
    }
```

Listing 5-15 is far from a comprehensive implementation of a Mediator Pattern; however, we're simply illustrating how this may be used to fulfil the OCP within an application.

Note   As with many of these techniques, what we're actually doing is reducing, rather than eliminating completely, the amount of code that would need to be changed in the original class. Ultimately, you will need information or events from the class, and something may need to change – the target is to make that change as localized and trivial as possible.

The final technique that we'll look at is injection.

Injection

In fact, injection, while being a way to extend functionality, is often seen as not only something to avoid but something to actively prevent. The principle here is that you ask your code to execute something and then pass that thing in, in the form of code.

Security

Unless you've been living under an IT rock for the last 25 years, you will likely have come across the concept of **SQL injection**, joined now in the OWASP top 10 by its close cousin **JavaScript injection**. Let's quickly review what these are, and then we can talk about how we might leverage the concept of injection without exposing ourselves to risk.

We'll start with SQL Injection, as it's perhaps the best-known attack vector, and this is simply because it's so easy to exploit. Let's take the code in Listing 5-16 as an example.

Listing 5-16. SQL Injection Vulnerability

```
void RunQuery(string value)
{
    string sql = "SELECT * FROM MY_TABLE WHERE SOME_VALUE = '" +
value + "'";
}

RunQuery("test");
```

As you can see from Listing 5-16, we're executing a fairly innocuous SQL query, and to make our function reusable, we're allowing the parameter to be passed in. The call to **RunQuery** is calling the query with a single parameter. However, let's imagine that **RunQuery** was being called with a value that came from outside the running program. SQL, like JavaScript, is dynamic, and so it will run anything you ask it. Imagine that the following string was passed in instead:

RunQuery("'; SELECT * FROM USERS; --");

This would form a perfectly valid SQL statement, and the database engine would simply execute the first statement, followed by the second. The same is true of JavaScript injection; if an attacker can find a point in your website where you execute JavaScript (even unintentionally), then they can force the site to perform in a way that you hadn't anticipated.

Note   One other factor about the code in Listing 5-16 that's worth noting as a reason to avoid this type of syntax is that most RDBMSs will try to cache your queries for performance. If the code in Listing 5-16 gets called with three separate values, it will be interpreted as three separate queries and cached three times. This is known as **flooding the cache** – as these three queries are cached, the query cache fills up with slightly different versions of the same query and eventually becomes useless.

Now we've seen that injection can be bad; but as with all things, it's not entirely bad. The key point to the attack vectors that we have seen here is that they allow external input and so are vulnerable to an injection attack. However, if we structure our software in such a way that the code being executed is known and trusted code, we can pass code around, which gives us a lot of power (after all, any dynamic language is, essentially, executing injected code). Listing 5-17 shows an example of that being possible in C#.

Listing 5-17. Injecting a Method

```
static void Main(string[] args)
{
    DoTheThing(() => Console.WriteLine("Test"));
}
```

```
public static void DoTheThing(Action theThing)
{
    theThing.Invoke();
}
```

In fact, Listing 5-17 is not the only way to inject code: it is possible to simply pass in a string and have it compile using the Roslyn compiler and execute that code, or to switch to *dynamic* mode; however, this structure, allowing you to simply pass a method onto the code, finds a halfway house of flexibility versus security. You could also inject a class that adheres to a given interface.

Now that we've established what the possibilities are, let's have a look at our target architecture.

Target Architecture

Figure 5-2 illustrated the target architecture for the system. As you can see, each section of functionality is broken into modules, and then each raises an event, based on what has happened within that module.

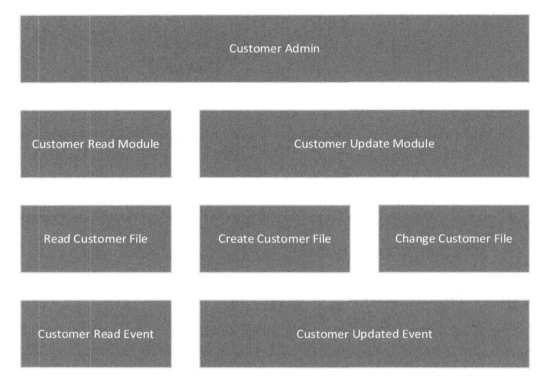

Figure 5-2. *Target architecture*

The principle here is that we will allow the events to be handled externally.

Before we delve into the method that we've chosen for extensibility, let's imagine what may be possible.

One way that we could achieve this is to allow the user to store, in our system, the code they'd like to handle the event – this would constitute the code *injection* that we mentioned earlier.

Another possibility would be to raise a message on a message bus. This doesn't really fit in this situation, as reacting to messages needs to be quite a rigid affair. We could. However, use the Mediator Pattern that we've discussed; this would work, although this may add an amount of complexity, in the form of the mediator itself, to our software.

The option that is left then is to provide a hook. Let's explore a little what that will look like; remember, our target is that changes need not result in changes to our software; that means (in an ideal world) that we shouldn't even have to change our software to load the extended functionality.

> **Note**   Remember that, as with everything we've discussed in this book, this is a trade-off again. Allowing users of the software to change the functionality without, even slightly, changing the base software provides a lot of flexibility and resilience; but you're adding complexity, and bugs in the external software may be difficult to find.

For our purposes, we'll provide a directory where the users can place libraries that contain the extended functionality.

Examples

The basis of this application, as with all the others, is going to be a .Net Console Application. However, the technique works equally well for a desktop (e.g., WinForms, WPF, or MAUI) or web applications. Depending on the type of application that you're dealing with, the specific approach may be more, or less, applicable; and you should always consider the comments that we've made around security.

As with other chapters, all the code can be found here:

`https://github.com/Apress/software-architecture-by-example`

Basic Functionality

The basic functionality of this application is a simple CRUD function (or at least the create and update part of that). As you can see from the architecture, the project is partitioned into the functional areas, as shown in Figure 5-3.

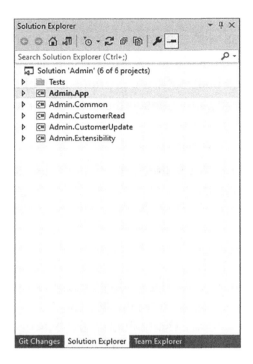

Figure 5-3. *Project structure*

For the basic functionality, we'll concentrate on the **App**, **Common**, **Update**, and **Read** modules. Let's start with the **App**. Listing 5-18 shows a simple menu system in the **Main** method.

Listing 5-18. Menu

```
static List<CustomerModel> _customers = new List<CustomerModel>();
static Random _rnd = new Random();
static Hook _hook = new Hook();

static void Main(string[] args)
{
    while (true)
    {
        Console.WriteLine("1 - Read Customer Data");
        Console.WriteLine("2 - Write Customer Data");
        Console.WriteLine("3 - Add Customer");
        Console.WriteLine("0 - Exit");
```

```
var choice = Console.ReadKey();
switch (choice.Key)
{
    case ConsoleKey.D0:
        return;

    case ConsoleKey.D1:
        ReadCustomerData();
        foreach (var customer in _customers)
        {
            Console.WriteLine($"Customer: {customer.
            Name}");
        }
        break;

    case ConsoleKey.D2:
        CommitCustomerData();
        break;

    case ConsoleKey.D3:
        ReadCustomerData();
        _customers.Add(new CustomerModel()
        {
            Name = $"Customer {Guid.NewGuid()}",
            Address = "Customer Address",
            CreditLimit = _rnd.Next(1000),
            Email = $"customer{_rnd.Next(10000)}
            @domain.com"
        });
        CommitCustomerData();

        break;

    }
  }
}
```

We won't dwell too deeply on the code in Listing 5-18, as it's relatively straightforward; the key things to note are that we have a **read**, **write**, and **add** function.

Let's now look at Listing 5-19, which shows the functionality behind the **Read** and **Write/Commit** methods.

Listing 5-19. Read and Commit

```
private static void ReadCustomerData()
{
    var read = new ReadService();
    _customers = read.ReadAll(@"c:\tmp\test.txt").ToList();
}

private static void CommitCustomerData()
{
    var write = new WriteService();
    write.Write(_customers, @"c:\tmp\test.txt");

    // Provide hook
    string jsonParams = JsonSerializer.Serialize(_customers);

    _hook.CreateHook(
        methodName: "After",
        className: "CommitCustomerData",
        parameters: new[] { jsonParams });
}
```

The main thing to note about Listing 5-19 is the call to **_hook.CreateHook**. We'll come back to this in the next section, but for now, we just need to make a mental note that this is the extensibility hook.

We won't look at **Admin.Common**, as it simply contains a shared model.

Note   In fact, there is a compelling argument against this method of passing data between modules; it tends to work well in a system such as this; however, as you'll see in the extended module, there are potentially preferable alternatives when dealing with external or distributed systems.

From Listing 5-19 to Listing 5-20, we could see that we were making use of a *ReadService* and *WriteService*. These are in the **CustomerRead** and **CustomerUpdate** modules, respectively.

Listing 5-20 shows the **CustomerRead** module.

Listing 5-20. Admin.CustomerRead.ReadService

```
public class ReadService : IReadService
{
    public CustomerModel Read(string dataFile, string customerName)
    {
        var customers = ReadAllRecords(dataFile);
        return customers.FirstOrDefault(a => a.Name == customerName);
    }

    public IEnumerable<CustomerModel> ReadAll(string dataFile) =>
        ReadAllRecords(dataFile);

    private IEnumerable<CustomerModel> ReadAllRecords(string dataFile)
    {
        string customerData = File.ReadAllText(dataFile);
        var customers = JsonSerializer.Deserialize<IEnumerable<Customer
        Model>>(customerData);
        return customers;
    }
}
```

In Listing 5-20, we see a very basic service that reads from a serialized data stream. Listing 5-21 shows the **WriteService**: essentially the counter function to the read; again, it's a very simple implementation.

Listing 5-21. Admin.CustomerUpdate.WriteService

```
public class WriteService : IWriteService
{
    public void Write(IEnumerable<CustomerModel> customers,
    string file)
    {
```

```
        string serialisedCustomers = JsonSerializer.
        Serialize(customers);
        File.WriteAllText(file, serialisedCustomers);
    }
}
```

We've now seen the basic functionality in these three modules. In Listing 5-19, we placed the hook into the code, so all we need to do now is to attach to that hook.

Extensibility

In **Admin.Extensibility**, we have what is essentially a helper method. Listing 5-19 shows this being called where data is committed, and Listing 5-22 shows the **CreateHook** method that we used.

Listing 5-22. CreateHook

```
public void CreateHook([CallerMemberName]string methodName = null,
string className = null, object[] parameters = null)
{
    // If className is not supplied then attempt to infer it
    if (string.IsNullOrWhiteSpace(className))
    {
        var stackTrace = new StackTrace();
        className = stackTrace.GetFrame(1).GetMethod().
        GetType().Name;
    }

    // Check that we have the basic arguments
    if (string.IsNullOrWhiteSpace(methodName) || string.
    IsNullOrWhiteSpace(className))
    {
        throw new ArgumentException("className and methodName
        cannot be null or empty");
    }
```

```
string executingPath = Assembly.GetExecutingAssembly().
Location;
string libraryFullPath = Path.Combine(Path.GetDirectoryName(
executingPath), $"{className}Extended.dll");

var library = Assembly.LoadFile(libraryFullPath);

foreach (Type type in library.GetExportedTypes())
{
    var c = Activator.CreateInstance(type);
    type.InvokeMember(methodName, BindingFlags.InvokeMethod,
    null, c, parameters);
}
}
```

Since this is the crux of the functionality, let's delve into this a little. The method itself accepts three parameters: the method name that should be called (this defaults to the method name that *made* the call), the class name (which forms part of the expected assembly name), and any parameters that need to be passed. Should we call the method as follows:

CreateHook("Method1", "Class1", null)

then the method would attempt to find an assembly in the current executing path, called **Class1Extended.dll**.

If the assembly was found, it would then attempt to execute a method called **Method1** on each class in that assembly; we've set the parameters to null, and so no parameters would be passed.

Note   Clearly, there may be issues with executing the method on every class. If this did prove to be an issue, it could be dealt with by a convention-based approach; perhaps you would only execute the method on the class with the **className**, or something similar.

In our case, we pass the method name as **"After"**, and the class name is set to **"CommitCustomerData"**; we also pass a serialized version of the data store through.

Note   Whether or not you manage such extensions yourself, you should probably treat the hook as an external system: don't trust anything that it returns (i.e., encode) and don't send it more information than is absolutely necessary. In this example, we are passing much more information than is necessary for the purpose of illustration and convenience.

There are many different ways to approach this problem; .Net allows several approaches, and depending on how strictly you wish to adhere to the OCP, you may use differing approaches.

Now that we've seen the basic functionality, along with the code for the hook, let's look into the extended functions.

Custom Functionality

Inside the main code directory of the repo (assuming that you've pulled it down) are three directories; **src** and **test** are the usual standard ones, but there is an additional one called **extended**. This contains a completely separate .Net solution, as shown in Figure 5-4.

Figure 5-4. *Directory structure*

The code inside this solution is shown in Listing 5-23.

Listing 5-23. CommitCustomerData Extension Class

```
public class CommitCustomerData
{
    public void After(string parameter)
    {
        Console.WriteLine(parameter);
```

```
using var doc = JsonDocument.Parse(parameter);
var element = doc.RootElement;

foreach (var eachElement in element.EnumerateArray())
{
    string name = eachElement.GetProperty("Name").GetString();
    decimal creditLimit = eachElement.
    GetProperty("CreditLimit").GetDecimal();

    if (creditLimit > 300)
    {
        Console.WriteLine($"{name} has a credit limit in excess
        of £300!");
    }
}
    }
  }
}
```

Again, let's break this down. The first thing to note is that we are not trying to deserialize the data. We can't have any dependency on the core code base whatsoever, and so we cannot share or rely on the structure of the JSON; as a result, we just treat it like a string and manually parse it. As stated earlier, this can be considered a better practice, depending on your use case.

Once we've parsed the data, we simply iterate and display a warning where the credit limit is greater than a given amount. This is compiled to a .Net Assembly and then simply copied into the output directory of the main project. We can then change this functionality without ever touching the core code base.

Summary

We have now finally looked at the SOLID principles, specifically focusing on the **Open-Closed Principle**. I like to think that once you've spent time thinking about such principles, you find that your code simply looks better and becomes more extensible. Much like the practice of test-driven development, after some time, even if you stop writing the tests first, the code is still written as though you were.

Writing extensible software is something that every software engineer is expected to do; however, what this means can vary hugely. The example that we've given in this chapter, of allowing the user of the software to extend it, is an extreme case; however, the principles that we've discussed can work across the extensible spectrum.

We should also consider that making something extensible often opens up a security vulnerability. We can often mitigate such vulnerabilities, but we need to realize that they are there and have a feel for the potential damage they can do to our system.

CHAPTER 6

The Travel Rep Problem

While writing this, I'm based in the United Kingdom – it's a common pastime here to complain about our broadband connectivity (even more than the weather these days); especially if, like me, you live away from a town center. You might be reading this in Mumbai, or Minneapolis, or Sydney, or London; if so, you probably have relatively good broadband too. However, not every part of the world does, nor do they have telephone reception.

Because I live outside of the city, when I commute in for work, I travel through a couple of areas of extremely bad reception, and so I lose my Internet connectivity. Sometimes, during these journeys, I'll try to use an application, either on my phone or laptop. What I *hope* will happen here is that I can use the application offline, much as a travel (or holiday representative) might, and then, when I enter an area of better connectivity, the application would simply synchronize the state.

In this chapter, we'll be discussing how we might design a system that is resilient to changes in Internet connectivity, even where the entire purpose of the application that is being designed is to retrieve and update information on a remote server.

© Paul Michaels 2022
P. Michaels, *Software Architecture by Example*, https://doi.org/10.1007/978-1-4842-7990-8_6

Background

Our client, **Lunar Polly Travel** (who you may remember from Chapter 3), was so impressed with the work that we did on their space travel system that they have asked us to look into another problem that they have: this time with their travel representatives.

The launch sites for their lunar space travel trips are dotted around the globe, although they tend (for obvious reasons) to be away from populated areas. The result is that the mobile reception is usually sketchy at best. The travel reps need to communicate to the head office when a flight is cancelled (typically due to weather), if a guest has a problem or complaint, and to simply check in to the launch site (so that head office knows where the reps are – as they frequently travel between sites within their allocated area).

Requirements

Although **Lunar Polly Travel** is now an existing customer, the requirements are new. You meet with the managing director again, and he gives the following requirements for the system:

The travel reps need an application that is able to:

- Provide a "check-in" at their current location.

- Create and issue a flight cancellation report.

- Create and issue a complaint form.

However, the main requirement here is that the system be capable of dealing with a situation where the connection to the Internet is either non-existent or intermittent.

We'll need to be clear on exactly what the MD expects to happen here. If the application is unable to make contact with the Internet and transmit these details, then it should be able to transmit the details the next time the device is online; however, the time and date should be recorded.

For example, let's imagine our travel rep is in Australia; and he starts in Carnarvon, WA, but is unable, for whatever reason, to get a reception until he reaches Lancelin, WA. Even though there was no reception, the central log should show each location in the correct order, with the correct time:

03/05/2021 - 15:20: Carnarvon, WA

05/05/2021 – 12:09: Lancelin, WA

Even though both updates may have been uploaded on the latter date.

Options

While the functional requirements here are important, the thing that we're going to focus on in this chapter is the non-functional requirement that we be able to operate both in a connected and a disconnected manner. This isn't just an issue for travel representatives working for mythical space travel companies: there are still large parts of the world that have very sketchy access to an Internet connection.

As we'll no doubt be familiar with by now, our first take on this will be to consider what this problem would look like were we to try to solve it without the aid of technology.

Manual Process

Our functional requirements here are relatively basic. Should we wish to imagine a manual version, we might call to mind a salesman in an Alfred Hitchcock film: when he arrived at a new location, he would "send a telegram." Our rep could do a similar thing: either by mail or by telephone, to alert the head office that he'd arrived and to state where he was.

For the flight cancellation report, we can imagine that this would be an urgent report telephoned into the head office; they would ensure that anyone booked onto the flight was alerted and refunded.

The complaint form might be a slightly different process. While the complaint form may be phoned in, we can imagine that this and the documentation accompanying the flight cancellation would sit in our travel rep's suitcase until they returned to the head office and handed the document in themselves.

That explains the manual process, but let's follow this analogy a little further. Since the areas that they are visiting have little reception, our travel rep struggles to get a phone signal, as well as an Internet one. As a result, they must travel to the regional office to make the call or wait until they have reception. This means that they either need to leave to make a round trip to the regional office or have to remember to keep trying to contact the head office.

We could imagine that providing our rep with an assistant may help with such things. The assistant to the travel rep could act in one of two ways: the travel rep could pass on information and ask the assistant to do something with it; for example, hand the assistant a complaint form and specifically ask them to drive that to the head office. The advantage here is that the travel rep can continue with their current task, while the assistant makes the drive. However, we can imagine a slightly different relationship: one where the travel rep treats their assistant as a proxy to the head office, rather than asking the assistant to do specific things, to simply treat the assistant as though they *were* the head office, giving them updates, handing them documents, etc. It would then be the responsibility of the assistant to deal with the head office as they saw fit.

Let's see how we might translate this to a technical solution.

Caching

The simplest solution, from an architectural standpoint, would be to have the application that the travel rep is using cache the data. From our manual approach, this would be very similar to the act of them putting the complaint form in their suitcase. Essentially, the application would maintain a local data store, which could be transferred when they got to the head office.

The main advantage of this approach is that it's incredibly simple. You maintain the state of the application locally – perhaps in a text file or small database.

One disadvantage here is that our application needs to maintain and update this cache – which is really not what the app should be doing; for example, what should happen if the file becomes corrupt or isn't there; these are things that the app shouldn't really be concerned with.

Another disadvantage is the methodology around synchronizing this file: when to do so, and how to do so. If we decide to only update at the head office, then there's a time delay; if we decide to update prior to that, then we need to build some form of polling logic into the app.

Let's look at a couple of patterns that may help with our predicament: the Sidecar Pattern and the Ambassador Pattern.

Sidecar Pattern

The Sidecar Pattern is, essentially, the concept that you would have a separate process that lives with your main process, but is local to it (Figure 6-1). This second (or sidecar) process is responsible for the parts of the application that need to perform a task that is not directly related to the primary function of the application.

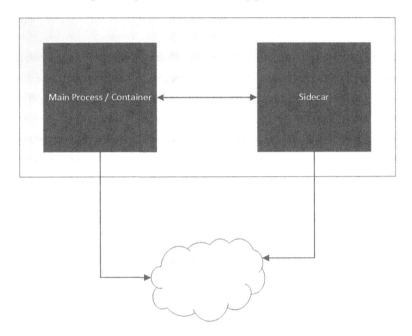

Figure 6-1. *Sidecar Pattern*

Let's consider the concept of logging: this is not central to any given business process; if there's an issue in writing a log, it's very unlikely that the required functionality would be that the main application fails. Introducing a **sidecar** to handle the logging means that all the logs are written out of process.

This pattern is used very often with containers: essentially allowing a container to perform its main function and then passing off any secondary functionality to a **sidecar**. In practice, the sidecar is accessed via an HTTP call to **localhost**.

Now that we've talked about what a sidecar is, how could it help us with our problem? Well, we may consider that, for example, the filing of a complaint report could go into a sidecar. This has the advantage that we no longer need to concern the main application with the transmission of the complaint – we just pass it to the sidecar and carry on. However, the complaint is part of the main functionality of the application; it's not like logging, where the functionality is peripheral.

The sidecar does seem like a possible solution, but let's investigate a variant of this pattern, known as the **Ambassador Pattern**.

Ambassador Pattern

The **Ambassador Pattern** (sometimes called the **Proxy Pattern**) is very similar to the **Sidecar Pattern**, in that it allows the main process to offload some of its work to a separate process. However, it differs in that in the **Ambassador Pattern**, the secondary process acts as an ambassador to the outside world.

We can think of a real-life ambassador; let's say the Norwegian Ambassador to Denmark. If Norway wants to communicate with Denmark, they would do that through their ambassador; the same is true for our service: when our service wishes to communicate with the outside world, it does so via the ambassador (Figure 6-2).

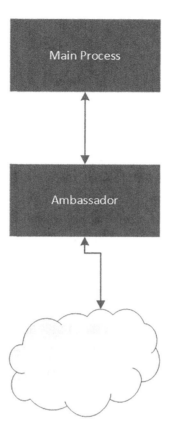

Figure 6-2. *Ambassador Pattern*

We may wonder what the advantage of such a pattern is, especially since the Sidecar Pattern seems to go most of the way. Well, let's consider our use case: we want our data to be sent to a central hub; however, we are unsure when we will be able to make the connection. We've already said that it seems like a bad design for our primary service to be concerned with such things, and so it could offline this onto a sidecar; however, instead of this, we could offload this onto an ambassador.

Changing our thinking like this means that our service doesn't need to think about what is being communicated: we simply call the ambassador (or proxy) and pass it the information; we can then be assured that at an appropriate point, the information will be transferred, but since we're going via a proxy, we can treat this as though we were communicating directly.

Both the Sidecar and Ambassador patterns are common in a microservice architecture. Since we are using them for a purpose other than this type of architecture, the details of this are not directly relevant, but it may help with context if we spend a short time discussing why that might be.

Microservices and Containers

The **Sidecar Pattern** specifically has become a very popular design pattern in container-based microservice architectures. There are a number of reasons for this, and we've already addressed some of the problems that the pattern can solve. It fits very well with the concept of containers because it means that a single container can offload its non-essential workload. Kubernetes, for example, allows for a Pod to have more than one container – this being the primary use for such a feature. The Pod (the main process and sidecar) live, die, and scale together.

Note   It is beyond the scope of this book to talk about containers or container orchestrators in any detail; this section is purely here for some context, as these patterns are most frequently used (at least at the time of writing) in connection with Kubernetes and container technologies.

The **Ambassador Pattern** is exactly the same idea; the only difference is one of concepts – the physical architecture of both is the same; that is to say that while the two may have different services and be called in different ways, they would both live in a second container within the same Pod.

Now that we've covered the options that we have, let's talk about our target architecture.

Target Architecture

We've spoken about the idea of using the Ambassador Pattern: a very basic version of which may be that we simply deploy a desktop application onto the target machine, and then have a service sitting on the same machine that all the communications go through. While this is a very simple and straightforward implementation, it does not make for a particularly simple deployment model.

Since the pattern that we are trying to use works well with containers, we could simply use that mechanism in order to deploy our software. As we'll be used to by now, there's no free lunch, but we'll talk about the trade-off later on.

Containers

If you search the Internet for containers, you'll see a number of images of cartoon shipping containers and a lot of talk of a tool called Docker.

Before we get into an explanation of what containers are, I'll take you back 20 or so years to my first job as a programmer (I promise the relevance will reveal itself shortly). I was asked to create an application (at the time, I believe the language was either Visual Basic 5 or Visual Basic 6). The program worked fine on my machine; however, when I sent the executable over to the customer, an error was displayed. I don't remember the error, but I've since established that what caused the error was that the target machine didn't have the VB runtime libraries.

We can now fast-forward a few years to an early CI/CD pipeline that I was involved in creating. This pipeline was essentially a DOS batch file that ran after code was checked in. It set up and configured a virtual machine in order to run some tests against the running code. This whole process worked well; however, setting up a virtual machine each time took a good 20 minutes from start to finish. The problem with a time of 20 minutes is that it's long enough that you would start on another task: if one of the tests failed, it would then be necessary to switch back and fix the broken test.

These two, seemingly unrelated, stories reveal a requirement for something a little like a virtual machine (in order to encapsulate all the dependencies that a program may have), but that has a smaller footprint (so that setting one up from scratch doesn't take 20 minutes). The answer could very well be a container. We can imagine a container as a mini virtual machine, but one where the operating system (or at least a full version of it) is omitted.

With this in mind, let's have a look what our target architecture for this system might look like.

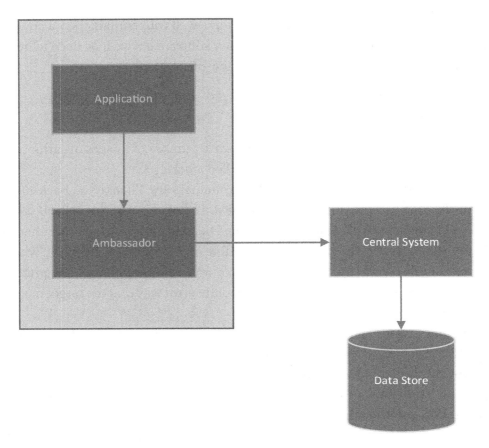

Figure 6-3. *Target architecture*

Figure 6-3 illustrates our target architecture. When we look at this diagram, there is one glaring point that we must address; let's imagine that while trying to update the data store, the central system fails. In a conventional system, the user would simply be informed that their update had failed and perhaps be given a support number to call. However, in our case, the user does not get informed of this, because the ambassador has already informed the main app that it will deal with the request.

Examples

There are, of course, dozens of ways to achieve this type of design; however, the particular one that we'll go for here makes use of an open source application called Hangfire:

https://github.com/HangfireIO/Hangfire

Hangfire is a library that allows you to configure delayed and repeated tasks in ASP.NET.

The source code for this, and all the code in this book, can be found here:

https://github.com/Apress/software-architecture-by-example

Project Structure

In our sample solution, we will have three projects.

Figure 6-4 illustrates the three projects that we have in our solution. In fact, the **TravelRep.CentralApi** is the odd one out here. The other two live together and form our solution, but the Central API mimics the API that we're trying to communicate with. Let's start with that.

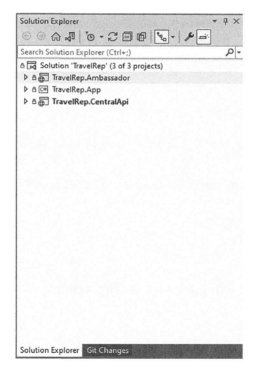

Figure 6-4. *Project structure*

TravelRep.CentralApi

As we've said, the Central API represents the central system that we're attempting to communicate with. In fact, the code for this, especially with the .Net 6 minimal API structure, is very concise. Listing 6-1 shows all the code necessary to create an API in .Net 6.

Listing 6-1. CentralApi

```
var builder = WebApplication.CreateBuilder(args);

builder.Services.AddEndpointsApiExplorer();
builder.Services.AddSwaggerGen();

var app = builder.Build();

if (app.Environment.IsDevelopment())
{
    app.UseSwagger();
    app.UseSwaggerUI();
}

app.UseHttpsRedirection();

app.MapPost("/checkin", async (double longitude, double latitude) =>
{
    Console.Write($"\n\n/checkin called: {DateTime.Now}\n\n\n");

    await ChaosMonkey();
    return Results.Ok();
});

app.MapPost("/cancellation", async (string report, int flightNumber) =>
{
    await ChaosMonkey();
    return Results.Ok();
});
```

```
app.MapPost("/complaint", async (string complaint) =>
{
    await ChaosMonkey();
    return Results.Ok();
});

app.Run();
```

This minimal API syntax doesn't fit every scenario, but in a situation like this, where we have very little code, it reduces the boiler plate code that we need down to the bare bones. In these lines of code, we use **MapPost** to specify the Http Verb that we will expose, along with the route to expose it on; for example, we're exposing an endpoint called /**checkin** as an **Http Post**.

Inside the code, you'll notice that we call a function called **ChaosMonkey** and then return OK (or HTTP code 200).

Let's talk a bit about what the **ChaosMonkey** function does, and the Chaos Monkey concept in general.

Chaos Monkey

The idea of a Chaos Monkey was invented by Netflix in 2011. Typically, the idea behind such **Chaos Engineering** tools is to introduce failure into the system intentionally.

Let's imagine that you've created a system, a complex system, but a working system. That system should be tolerant to failure: while your system may work today, tomorrow you might have a power failure that brings down your main server. Chaos Engineering allows us to guard against such failures by forcing them to be commonplace. If we know that failure will happen eventually, then waiting until that failure happens naturally at 3 a.m. seems like a missed opportunity; if you build failure into your system, your engineers will be building fault-tolerant systems; otherwise, eventually, the systems *will* fail; you just won't have control over when and how.

In our case, our Chaos Monkey is a little tool that forces our **CentralApi** to randomly fail in three separate ways.

Listing 6-2. ChaosMonkey

```
Random _random = new Random();

async Task ChaosMonkey()
{
    Console.WriteLine($"\n\nChaosMonkey Invoked: {DateTime.Now}");

    int result = _random.Next(5);
    switch (result)
    {
        case 0:
            Console.WriteLine($"Throw exception immediately");
            throw new Exception("Failure");

        case 1:
            Console.WriteLine($"Wait, then throw exception");
            await Task.Delay(3000);
            throw new Exception("Failure");

        case 2:
            Console.WriteLine($"Wait, then work");
            await Task.Delay(3000);
            break;
    }
    Console.WriteLine("Call succeeded");
}
```

In Listing 6-2, we see that we're selecting a random number between 0 and 4. For three of those numbers, we introduce a level of failure: meaning that for two in five times, the call will complete without incident.

Our levels of failure are that the call is delayed, fails, or is delayed and then fails. This failure rate seems very high and is probably much worse than our target system; however, it's always best practice to assume your software is working in a far more hostile environment than it is.

Now that we've covered the Central System API, let's discuss the main application.

TravelRep.App

The **TravelRep.App** is the client's user interface. It's built inside a container. We'll delve into more detail on that in the "Containers" section; but here, we'll have a very quick look at the code inside this application; we won't cover the entire application, as some of it is there for the purposes of testing.

Let's look at one of the client methods in the **Program.cs** file.

Listing 6-3. Client Application

```
var httpFactory = serviceProvider.GetRequiredService<IHttpClient
Factory>();
var httpClient = httpFactory.CreateClient();
httpClient.BaseAddress = new Uri(systemConfiguration.
AmbassadorBaseUrl);

var location = new TravelRep.App.Location()
{
    Latitude = 12,
    Longitude = 256
};
Console.WriteLine("\n\nCalling checkin API...");
var content = new StringContent(JsonSerializer.Serialize(location),
Encoding.UTF32, "application/json");
var result = await httpClient.PostAsync("checkin", content);
result.EnsureSuccessStatusCode();

Console.WriteLine("Reading results...");
var results = await result.Content.ReadAsStringAsync();
Console.WriteLine(results);
```

The code in Listing 6-3 is, essentially, code that we've seen before. It's not particularly noteworthy, with the exception of the HttpClient Base Address. Instead of trying to communicate with an outside system, we're making a call to the ambassador; Listing 6-4 shows the **appsettings.json** that this setting comes from.

Listing 6-4. AppSettings.json

```
{
  "Logging": {
    "LogLevel": {
      "Default": "Information",
      "Microsoft.AspNetCore": "Warning"
    }
  },
  "AllowedHosts": "*",
  "AmbassadorBaseUrl": "http://ambassador-api"

}
```

The important setting from Listing 6-4 is the **AmbassadorBaseUrl**; this is set to an internal docker compose reference. We'll look in more detail at the docker compose file in the following section relating to containers. We've covered everything that we need to know from the application itself: we make an HTTP call, but instead of trying to contact the outside world, we simply call the ambassador and carry on. As far as our application is concerned, it's made the call, and the user can continue to use the application.

Let's move on to discuss the Ambassador project.

TravelRep.Ambassador

The Ambassador project, as we've discussed, is essentially a proxy between our application and the outside world; however, it does need quite a lot of functionality; for example, if the application calls the ambassador and the ambassador isn't able to pass that call on, what should it do? In our example, as we've discussed, we'll be using a third-party, open source tool, called Hangfire, to handle that complexity.

The GitHub repository is here:

```
https://github.com/HangfireIO/Hangfire
```

We'll talk in much more detail about Hangfire and how it works in the next section, but let's see how we're handling one of the calls from the client application.

Listing 6-5. Ambassador Endpoint

```
app.MapPost("/checkin", async ([FromBody]Location location,
ICentralSystemProxyService centralSystemProxyService, IHttpClientFactory
httpClientFactory) =>
{
    var result = await centralSystemProxyService.CallCheckin(location.
    Longitude, location.Latitude);
    if (result) return Results.Ok();
    return Results.Accepted();
});
```

In Listing 6-5, we can see how we're handling a single call; if you wish to see the others, then I'd encourage you to download the code, but we'll just look at one for the sake of simplicity (as the architectural principle is the same for all the calls). In this endpoint, we're using an abstracted internal proxy to handle the actual logic of the call.

Listing 6-6. CentralSystemProxyService

```
    // Returns true for a successful call,
    // and false to indicate that it will continue to try
    public async Task<bool> CallCheckin(double longitude, double
    latitude)
    {
        Console.WriteLine($"CallCheckin({longitude}, {latitude})");
        var result = await CallCentralSystemCheckin(longitude,
        latitude);
        if (result) return true;

        BackgroundJob.Enqueue(() =>
            CallCentralSystemCheckinFireAndForget(longitude,
            latitude));

        return false;
    }
```

We've discussed the advantages of using proxies inside your code in previous chapters: they help with unit tests, and they can make the code more extensible and readable. In the method shown in Listing 6-6, we're making a call to **CallCentralSystemCheckin** – this method (shown in Listing 6-7) simply calls out to the central system and returns true if that call was successful. However, if the result from this call shows that the call couldn't be made (i.e., the central system was unavailable), then we add an item to the Hangfire queue (we'll come back to this in the next section on Hangfire itself).

Listing 6-7. CallCentralSystemCheckin

```
public async Task<bool> CallCentralSystemCheckin(double longitude,
double latitude)
{
    try
    {
        var client = _httpClientFactory.CreateClient();
        var content = new StringContent("");
        string query = $"?longitude={longitude}&latitude=
        {latitude}";
        var result = await client.PostAsJsonAsync($"{_
        systemConfiguration.CentralSystem}/checkin{query}",
        content);
        if (result.IsSuccessStatusCode) return true;

        var results = await result.Content.ReadAsStringAsync();
        _logger.LogWarning("Call failed:");
        _logger.LogWarning(results);
        return false;
    },
    catch (Exception ex)
    {
        _logger.LogError(ex, ex.Message);
        return false;
    }
}
```

Now that we've seen the basic logic, let's delve further into what Hangfire does for us, and how.

Hangfire

If our call to the central system fails, we need to try again; however, if we built that directly into client system, we would simply weigh it down with the burden of managing those future calls, likewise if we tried to build it directly into the API. We should also consider *when* we would like to make these calls; there's little point in repeatedly trying to do the same thing – if the call failed, then immediately trying again will likely fail again. What we need is a back-off mechanism.

Hangfire is a tool that allows us to execute an offline task at a time of our choosing. Since what we're doing is trying to execute a task at a future time and, where that fails, to try the same call again at increasing intervals – Hangfire fits the bill very well.

The setup for Hangfire itself is very straightforward, and we won't cover it in too much detail here. In order to use Hangfire in our project, we're importing four packages – shown in Listing 6-8.

Listing 6-8. Ambassador Project File

```xml
<ItemGroup>
        <PackageReference Include="Microsoft.VisualStudio.Azure.
        Containers.Tools.Targets" Version="1.14.0" />
        <PackageReference Include="Swashbuckle.AspNetCore"
        Version="6.2.3" />
        <PackageReference Include="Hangfire.AspNetCore"
        Version="1.7.27" />
        <PackageReference Include="Hangfire.Core"
        Version="1.7.27" />
        <PackageReference Include="Hangfire.LiteDB"
        Version="0.4.1" />
        <PackageReference Include="Hangfire.Dashboard.
        Authorization" Version="3.0.0" />
</ItemGroup>
```

From Listing 6-8, initially, we're only interested in the first three Hangfire packages; they allow us to use Hangfire and give us the storage engine to use. **LiteDB** is a very similar engine to **SQLite**, and allows us to store our Hangfire status in a single storage file with no installation consideration.

As far as such a process is necessary, we've now *set up* Hangfire. We'll now return to the code that we were examining in the previous section.

Listing 6-9. CentralSystemProxyService

```
// Returns true for a successful call,
// and false to indicate that it will continue to try
public async Task<bool> CallCheckin(double longitude, double
latitude)
{
    Console.WriteLine($"CallCheckin({longitude}, {latitude})");
    var result = await CallCentralSystemCheckin(longitude,
    latitude);
    if (result) return true;

    BackgroundJob.Enqueue(() =>
        CallCentralSystemCheckinFireAndForget(longitude, latitude));

    return false;
}

[AutomaticRetry(Attempts = 5, OnAttemptsExceeded =
AttemptsExceededAction.Fail,
    DelaysInSeconds = new[] { 1, 3, 20, 60, 3600 })]
public async Task CallCentralSystemCheckinFireAndForget(double
longitude, double latitude)
{
    Console.WriteLine($"CallCentralSystemCheckinFireAndForget(
    {longitude}, {latitude})");
    var result = await CallCentralSystemCheckin(longitude,
    latitude);
    if (result) throw new Exception("Unable to contact central
    system for checkin");
}
```

In Listing 6-9, we see again the **CallCheckin** method, but here we go further and examine the **CallCentralSystemCheckinFireAndForget** method (see Listing 6-7 for the **CallCentralSystemCheckin** method).

The fire-and-forget method wraps the main method but throws an exception where it fails. Hangfire treats this as a failed job and will reattempt it. The decorators at the top of the method – **AutomaticRetry** – tell Hangfire when and how often to retry; for the purpose of demonstration, I've limited this to five retries: the first two almost instantly, then exponentially increasing, until the last retry waits a full hour. If this were a real system, we might settle on an hour and simply retry every hour until we got a success.

Enqueue and Schedule

There are two methods provided for the purpose of signaling to Hangfire that it should start a job: Enqueue, which simply tells Hangfire to execute the task as soon as it's ready, and Schedule, which allows the specification of a time delay or specific scheduled time (e.g., execute this task in ten minutes, or execute this task at 3 p.m.).

Persistence and Configuration

Since Hangfire manages your tasks offline, it must keep a record of those tasks. It does so in a persistence layer, which you can specify for it; in our case, we're using **LiteDB** (as we said earlier).

Listing 6-10. Program.cs - Add Hangfire to the Middleware Pipeline

```
var builder = WebApplication.CreateBuilder(args);
// Add services to the container.
// Learn more about configuring Swagger/OpenAPI at https://aka.ms/
aspnetcore/swashbuckle
builder.Services.AddEndpointsApiExplorer();
builder.Services.AddSwaggerGen();
builder.Services.AddHttpClient();
builder.Services.AddLogging();
```

```
builder.Services.AddHangfire(configuration =>
{
    configuration.UseLiteDbStorage("./hf.db");
});
builder.Services.AddHangfireServer();
```

In Listing 6-10, we see that we can specify the persistence engine when we add the Hangfire functionality to the middleware pipeline. The **UseLiteDbStorage** is a method provided by the **Hangfire.LiteDB** package, and there are sister methods for SQL Server, MySQL, Oracle, Mongo, Cosmos, and many other database engines. We're going to use the **LiteDB** option here, as we said, because it requires very little in the way of configuration.

We've now covered the basic functionality of Hangfire; like most useful tools, there's not a lot to it; it does one thing and does it well. Hangfire also provides a visual dashboard so that you can see what it's doing without delving into the database (which you can also do, but I feel that would be too much of a deep dive for this chapter).

Hangfire Dashboard

The Hangfire dashboard gives us a way to see exactly what is happening, how many jobs are executing, have failed, and are scheduled to be retried. Figure 6-5 shows an example of the Hangfire dashboard.

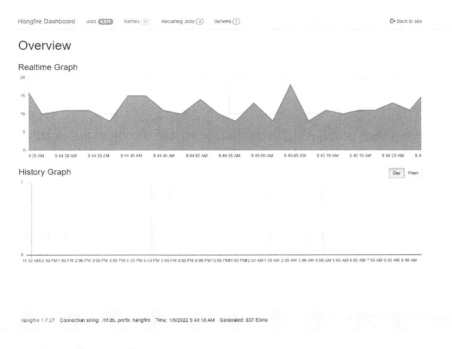

Figure 6-5. *Hangfire graph*

We'll talk later about how this is exposed from the container, but adding this functionality is relatively trivial, as we can see from Listing 6-11.

Listing 6-11. Program.cs – Adding Hangfire Dashboard

```
var options = new DashboardOptions()
{
    Authorization = new[] { new AuthorizationFilter() }
};
app.UseHangfireDashboard("/hangfire", options);
```

One thing to note from Listing 6-11 is the use of the **AuthorizationFilter**; in fact, this is necessitated by a quirk of using Hangfire from inside a container. You can use this to limit the access to the Dashboard, but for our example, we simply allow anyone to access the Dashboard (see Listing 6-12).

Listing 6-12. Program.cs – AuthorizationFilter

```
public class AuthorizationFilter : IDashboardAuthorizationFilter
{
    public bool Authorize(DashboardContext context) => true;
}
```

We've covered the Central API, the Ambassador, and the client application. What remains is to talk about the technical considerations of using containers in this context.

Containers

In this section, we'll talk about some of the features and quirks of Docker and Docker Compose, that we've either made use of, or circumvented.

Docker Compose

Docker Compose, is a tool, shipped with Docker, that allows for the configuration and deployment of multiple containers. Imagine a situation where you have a development environment that requires a database and three APIs running; you could configure Docker Compose to run all of these containers with a single command. However, the reason that we're discussing Docker Compose here is that by building our containers inside a single compose file, we get an internal network set up for us; that is, our client application can communicate with the Ambassador directly.

Listing 6-13. docker-compose.yml

```
version: '3'
services:
  ambassador-api:
    build: .\TravelRep.Ambassador
    ports:
      - "5010:80"
    logging:
      driver: "json-file"
```

```
main-app:
  build: .\TravelRep.App
  stdin_open: true
  tty: true
  depends_on:
    - "ambassador-api"
```

We can configure our services within the compose file with aliases; for example, in Listing 6-13, we reference the Ambassador API as **ambassador-api** and the client application as **main-app**. As you saw earlier, this means that within the **main-app**, we can call out to a URL of **http://ambassador-api**, and our call will be routed to the correct service.

We should also call attention to the **depends_on** section, which forces the creation of the service on which we depend, first.

In order to build our docker configuration, we would issue the following command:

docker compose build --no-cache

This essentially builds all of the services within the docker file. The **--no-cache** clause is optional and will take longer if you use it; however, if you're making changes, it will ensure that your changes are picked up.

Note   We will be using PowerShell to run Docker Compose commands. PowerShell commands are slightly different than if you were running this using a Linux terminal

---

In order to run the docker compose file, we can use the following command:

docker compose run main-app

In fact, a more traditional method of running a Docker Compose file would be to call

docker compose up

In the next section, we'll discuss why that isn't possible in our situation.

Displaying a UI

In our application, we are displaying an interactive user interface; admittedly, it's not a particularly complex one, but it does require that the user be able to interact with the docker container. In Listing 6-13, we can see the following switch:

```
stdin_open: true
tty: true
```

These allow our docker container to be interactive; however, on their own, they are insufficient. Just issuing a **docker compose up** will fail because docker compose cannot allow any containers with this flag to be interactive, as there may be more than one. Instead, we would issue the following command:

```
docker compose run main-app
```

In this instance, we have specifically told **docker compose** to run a specific container, and so it can now adhere to our interactive command. Because we have also told it that this container depends on the **ambassador-api**, the Docker engine will ensure that both are running correctly and allow us to communicate with the container as we would wish.

Since we are calling from inside of Docker to outside of Docker (i.e., the ambassador is calling the central service) on the same machine, there are a few more considerations.

Contacting the Host Machine from a Container

Were we not inside a container, contacting an API from another process on that machine would simply be a matter of referencing **localhost**. However, we have a problem in our case, which is that inside a container, **localhost** refers to the **localhost** of the container itself.

host.docker.internal

Figure 6-6 illustrates how this looks in practice.

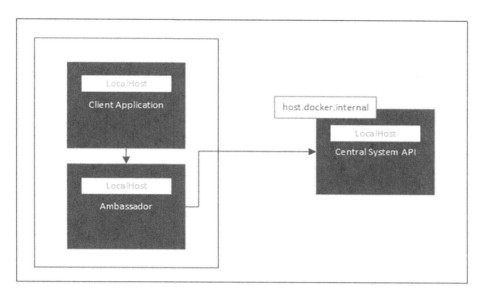

Figure 6-6. *Docker hosting*

As a result, as shown is Figure 6-6, if you wish to reference the host machine, you do so using the reference to **host.docker.internal**.

Configuring SSL/TLS

Before we discuss the certificates, let's remind ourselves of the specific setup that we have, with regard to Docker containers.

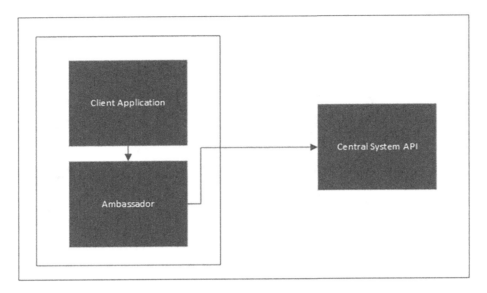

Figure 6-7. *Docker architecture*

Figure 6-7 illustrates the communication channels; the dividing boxes in this diagram are important to understand the problem that we face here.

Note   While it is important to understand the certificates and how we are intending to make them work locally, it's important to also understand that this is only an issue locally; in a production environment, we would need to generate or purchase a valid certificate based on a trusted certificate authority.

Indeed, you can create a .Net API locally, and call it from another .Net application, and have that API call another .Net application, and so forth ad infinitum; you will not get a certificate error because all of those instances would be running using a dev certificate. Indeed, you can force a dev certificate to be created in .Net by issuing the following command:

dotnet dev-certs https --trust

This will generate a self-signed certificate; see the following link for details:

https://docs.microsoft.com/en-us/dotnet/core/additional-tools/self-signed-certificates-guide

When you generate a development certificate like this, it gets placed in your personal certificates; you can view this (on a Windows machine) by running **certmgr**. Figure 6-8 shows the certificates.

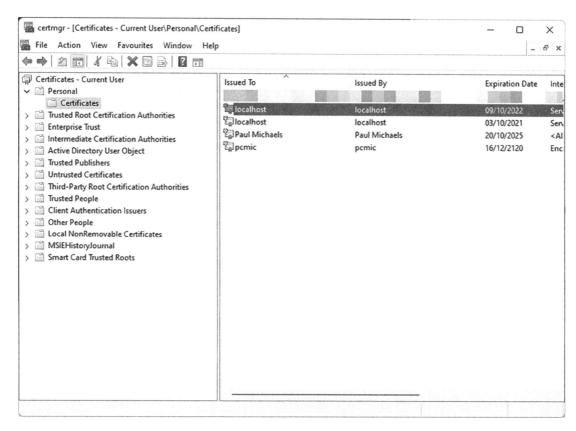

Figure 6-8. CertMgr

The final thing that's worth noting from Figure 6-8 is that the development certificate is issued to **localhost**; this will be relevant shortly.

We can delve even further into the certificate generated by opening the details (at the time of writing, and in Windows, that's a double click on the certificate). Figure 6-9 shows the certificate details.

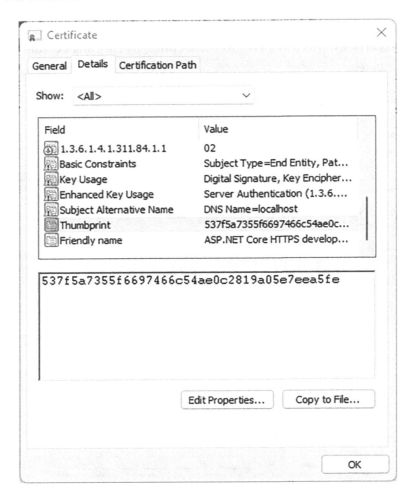

Figure 6-9. *Certificate details*

Perhaps the most interesting thing about Figure 6-9 is the Thumbprint; this dictates the unique identifier of the certificate; in order to be trusted, a certificate needs to match this thumbprint (or any thumbprint in the trusted certificates) or needs to derive from a trusted certificate authority.

Let's reconsider our architecture in this light: we have a development certificate for our **Central System API**; however, we're trying to access this endpoint from, what is in effect, a different machine; our container is Linux, and so it will not trust the development certificate for the **Central System API** any more than it would from an external server.

Further, our development certificate is for **localhost** (Figure 6-8), meaning that even if we were to have the same development certificate, it would not apply to **host.docker. internal**.

In order to get around this, we need to issue our own certificate. For this, we could use an open source tool called **OpenSSL**; you can find details on that tool here:

`www.openssl.org`

This is an excellent tool; however, for our purposes, it may introduce unnecessary complexity.

mkcert

Instead, we'll use a tool called **mkcert**; the following link is a blog post, written by the author, that illustrates the usage of this tool:

`https://blog.filippo.io/mkcert-valid-https-certificates-for-localhost`

The software is open source, and the repository is here:

`https://github.com/FiloSottile/mkcert`

Let's quickly run through how to set up the certificates such that you can run the project in a test environment (this assumes that you're running a Windows host and Linux containers).

Step 1. Install mkcert

On the host machine, install mkcert; you can do this using chocolatey, using the following command:

`choco install mkcert`

Note   There are other ways to install this, and I would encourage the reader to review both the blog post and repository listed for further information.

Step 2. Install the Trusted Root Certificate

Now that mkcert is installed, running the following command will create a trusted root certificate:

`mkcert -install`

This will generate a trusted root certificate. Figure 6-10 shows what that looks like.

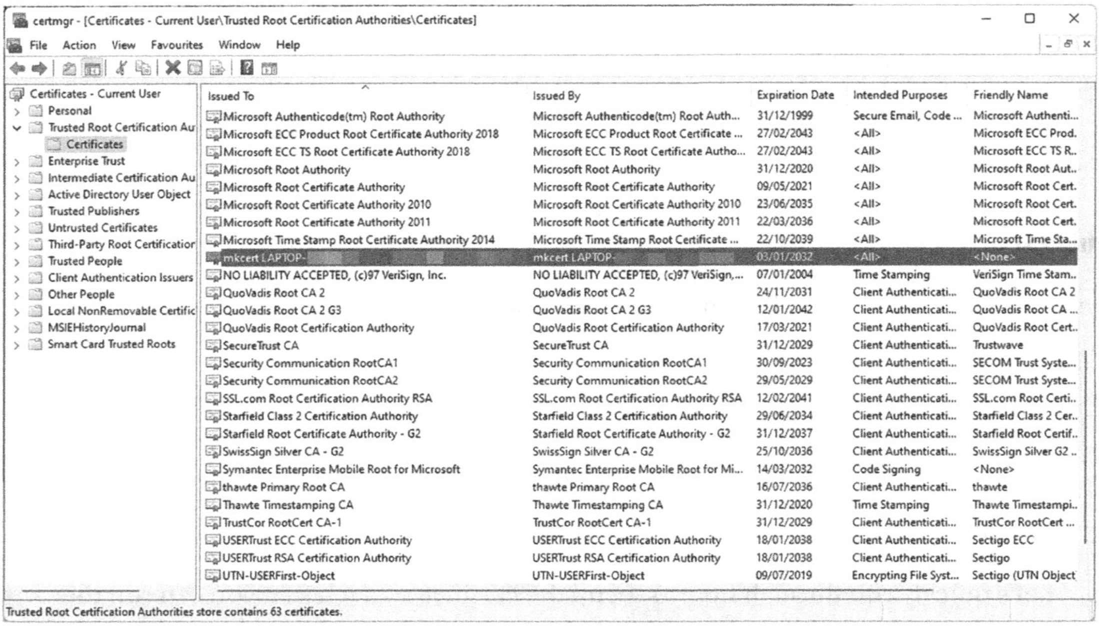

Figure 6-10. *mkcert root certificate*

In addition to creating the certificate, this will create the following files in the directory **%localappdata%\mkcert**:

```
rootCA.pem
rootCA-key.pem
```

What this means is that now any certificate mkcert creates will be implicitly trusted on this machine because it has a root certificate authority. In fact, our next step is to create such a certificate.

Step 3. Create a Certificate

With the **mkcert** command, we can pass a list of domains and have it generate a certificate for those domains, for example:

```
mkcert localhost host.docker.internal
```

This will create a certificate that works for both **localhost** and **host.docker.internal** domains. See Figure 6-11 for the expected output of this command.

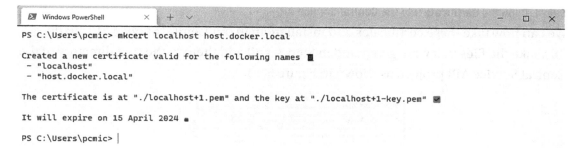

```
Windows PowerShell          ×    +  ∨                                    —   □   ×

PS C:\Users\pcmic> mkcert localhost host.docker.local

Created a new certificate valid for the following names ▮
 - "localhost"
 - "host.docker.local"

The certificate is at "./localhost+1.pem" and the key at "./localhost+1-key.pem" ☑

It will expire on 15 April 2024 ▪

PS C:\Users\pcmic> |
```

Figure 6-11. *mkcert*

These certificates are based on the root certificate authority that **mkcert** installed in Step 1, meaning that they will be trusted by the host machine. Figure 6-12 shows the newly created certificate chain; from this, we can see that the new certificate is linked to the trusted root certificate authority and will, therefore, be trusted.

Certificate   ×

General   Details   Certification Path

Certification path
┌──┐
│ 🖳 mkcert LAPTOP-▮▮▮▮▮▮ʾ\pcmic@LAPTOP-▮▮▮ ▮ (Paul Micha │
│   🖳 LAPTOP-   ʾ\pcmic@LAPTOP-   (Paul Michaels) │
└──┘

                                              View Certificate

Certificate status:
┌──┐
│ This certificate is OK.   │
│   │
│   │
└──┘

                                                      OK

Figure 6-12. *Certificate chain*

Now that we've created the certificate, we need to copy that into the correct place.

Step 4. Copy the Certificate into the Central Service API

We can now take these certificates and install them in our Central Service API. To do this, take the files that were generated in Step 3, and add them to the root directory of the Central Service API project, as shown in Figure 6-13.

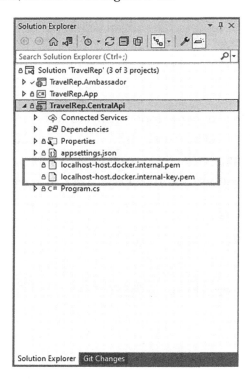

Figure 6-13. *Copy the certificate into the Central System API*

Once there, we can change the configuration, such that Kestrel (assuming we're self-hosting) will trust the certificate. Listing 6-14 illustrates the change to **appsettings.json**.

Listing 6-14. appsettings.json

```
{
  "Logging": {
    "LogLevel": {
      "Default": "Information",
      "Microsoft.AspNetCore": "Warning"
    }
  },
```

```
  "AllowedHosts": "*",
  "Kestrel": {
    "Certificates": {
      "Default": {
        "Path": "localhost-host.docker.internal.pem",
        "KeyPath": "localhost-host.docker.internal-key.pem"
      }
    }
  }
}
```

Step 5. Copy the Certificates to the Ambassador API

In the final step, we need to copy the root certificate over to the Ambassador project and then change the docker file so that we add **mkcert** as a trusted root authority on that container.

There are several ways to approach this, but the simplest is to download the mkcert executable and copy it across to the Ambassador project, along with the root certificate authority. See Figure 6-14 for an example.

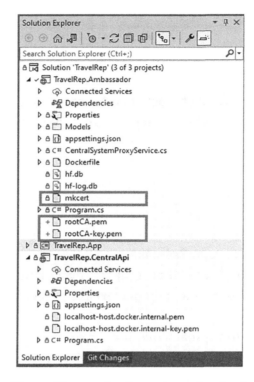

Figure 6-14. *Copy certificate files and mkcert into the Ambassador project*

The mkcert files can be downloaded from the following location:

https://github.com/FiloSottile/mkcert/releases

The final step is to change the Ambassador **dockerfile**. Listing 6-15 shows the new **dockerfile**.

Listing 6-15. Ambassador dockerfile

```
FROM mcr.microsoft.com/dotnet/aspnet:6.0 AS base
WORKDIR /app
EXPOSE 80
EXPOSE 443

FROM mcr.microsoft.com/dotnet/sdk:6.0 AS build
WORKDIR /src
```

```
COPY ["TravelRep.Ambassador.csproj", "TravelRep.Ambassador/"]
RUN dotnet restore "TravelRep.Ambassador/TravelRep.Ambassador.csproj"

WORKDIR /src/TravelRep.Ambassador/
COPY . .

RUN dotnet build "TravelRep.Ambassador.csproj" -c Release -o /app/build

FROM build AS publish
RUN dotnet publish "TravelRep.Ambassador.csproj" -c Release -o /app/publish

FROM base AS final
WORKDIR /app

COPY mkcert /usr/local/bin
COPY rootCA*.pem /root/.local/share/mkcert/
RUN chmod +x /usr/local/bin/mkcert \
   && mkcert -install \
   && rm -rf /usr/local/bin/mkcert

COPY --from=publish /app/publish .
ENTRYPOINT ["dotnet", "TravelRep.Ambassador.dll"]
```

The relevant section of Listing 6-15 copies the **mkcert** executable into **/usr/local/bin** and the root CA into **/root/.local/share/mkcert/**. When we call **mkcert -install**, this installs the root certificate authority that we've provided, meaning that the certificate in the Central System API will now be accepted as a valid certificate, as it was issued by this CA.

Durability

The final point that I'd like to make about these examples is around durability. While the containers are running, the system will remain reliable; that is, if the travel rep tries to send the messages to the central system, then the container will continue running and trying. However, once the container is stopped, this will cancel the outstanding jobs (effectively like shutting down a server that was running this). It's also worth remembering that containers are, or should be considered, ephemeral: meaning that you cannot rely on the state of the container remaining.

Summary

We have investigated the concept of creating an application that can deal with network outages and connectivity problems. For this, we used a piece of OSS called Hangfire; however, the concept of storing the state of a call locally is not something that is specific to that tool.

In this chapter, we've also investigated the concept of Chaos Engineering and how we can use that concept to make our software resilient to failure by introducing that failure intentionally. We've also discussed the **Sidecar** and **Ambassador** patterns, which both fit quite well into our specific problem but are also useful for certain types of cloud architecture.

Finally, we covered some specific **docker** and **docker compose** issues, especially with using certificates locally.

In this book, I have attempted to showcase (albeit some far-fetched but) real-life scenarios. All of the problems in this book are based on problems that are faced by software engineers and architects around the world on a daily basis.

If there's one message that I think I've tried to convey, it's that there are no absolutes; this isn't mathematics, and by that, I certainly do not mean that what we do is not complex, or difficult, or important; I mean that for a mathematician, there is a correct answer: 5 + 3 = 8 – that has always been true and will always be true, and there are no gray areas. In software engineering, that is not the case.

In my early career, I learned about relational databases. I learned what normalizing a database meant and why we should do it. Was this the *correct* way to store data? Absolutely not! It was, however, correct at the time; hard drives were measured in megabytes, not gigabytes, and certainly not terabytes; if you'd have suggested what is now called a NoSQL database at the time, the argument would have been that storing that much data would be prohibitively expensive.

Since hard drive space has become cheaper, people now undertake activities of denormalizing databases. There are still no absolutes; every time you make a decision involving a piece of software, you're making a decision that one thing matters more than another thing. That is always the case; for example, if you decide to choose to use event sourcing, as we explored in Chapter 2, you're exchanging hard drive space for context and accuracy of data. In Chapter 1, we talked about using message brokers – where we decided that we preferred a loosely coupled system but sacrificed speed of communication.

In Chapter 3, we decided that data integrity was the more important factor, again sacrificing speed. Chapter 4 saw us exchange speed for database read/write for data consistency.

We created a modular and extensible admin system in Chapter 5, but the price was development time. Finally, in this chapter, we have chosen reliability and speed of deployment over system speed and complete consistency.

All of the decisions that we made were both right and wrong at the same time; it depends on the use case – it depends on the customer. As you design your system, you should talk to the users of that system and discuss what they will use it for. Obviously, these conversations must be carefully framed; for example, if you hand a user a list of non-functional requirements (security, development speed, system speed, reliability, testability, cost, extensibility, etc.) and ask them to tick which they want, they will tick them all!

Questions around this topic should be around the usage. Let's use Chapter 2 as an example; clearly, if you ask a user whether they want data to be accurate, they'll tell you they do; the very question will lose their confidence in your ability; however, if you ask them about the budget and the potential impact that storing a given amount of data will have, you can explain that there is a consequence to storing that level of data. In the end, you may both decide that the cost is trivial in comparison to the benefits, or the cost of the project may be the main consideration for the client.

Finally, I would suggest that, having made such a decision, you document that you have done so; you may do this in an email, or a document, or even in the code itself in the form of an **Architectural Decision Record**.

Thank you for reading this book, and I wish you every success in your future projects.

APPENDIX A

Technical Appendix

Throughout this book, I've tried to keep the focus on the specific code that relates to the architectural principle in question. If each chapter had reams and reams of code covering a lot of the plumbing code, it would detract from the subject matter. Consequently, most of the code that would be necessary for a simulation to actually run has been omitted from the chapters themselves. All of this code can be found here, in the GitHub repo:

```
https://github.com/Apress/software-architecture-by-example
```

This appendix covers sections of code that were too bulky or tangential to make sense inside the chapters themselves.

Chapter 1

This section will cover the creation of the third-party API proxy that we used in the chapter.

Let's start with the third-party APIs (in fact, for our purposes, we will only need one, although we should bear in mind that there will be more).

We'll start by creating a directory for our code (Listing A-1).

Listing A-1. Terminal – Create Directory for the Chapter and the API

```
mkdir software-architecture-by-example
cd software-architecture-by-example
mkdir booking-api
```

© Paul Michaels 2022
P. Michaels, *Software Architecture by Example*, https://doi.org/10.1007/978-1-4842-7990-8

Now that we have a directory, we can create our API project (Listing A-2).

Listing A-2. Terminal – Create New API Project

```
dotnet new api
```

This gives us the default Weather Forecast API. Let's first rename a couple of files:
WeatherForecastController.cs to ***ExternalTicketBooking.cs***
WeatherForecast.cs to ***TicketInformation.cs***
We'll start with the contents of the file ***TicketInformation.cs*** (Listing A-3).

Listing A-3. Code – TicketInformation.cs

```
using System;

namespace booking_api
{
    public class TicketInformation
    {
        public string EventCode { get; set; }

        public DateTime EventDate { get; set; }

        public decimal Price { get; set; }

        public string SeatCode { get; set; }

        public int Quantity { get; set; }

    }
}
```

This is simply a class to hold the ticket information and will be serialized and passed back to the caller as a JSON object. The only other thing that we'll need to do to create our mock API is to create a controller (shown in Listing A-4); I've added mine to a **Controllers** subdirectory.

Listing A-4. Code – ExternalTicketBookingController.cs

```
using System;
using System.Collections.Generic;
using System.Threading.Tasks;
using Microsoft.AspNetCore.Mvc;
```

200

```
namespace booking_api.Controllers
{
    [ApiController]
    [Route("[controller]/[action]")]
    public class ExternalTicketBookingController : ControllerBase
    {
        private static Random _random = new Random();
        private static int _capacity = 1200000;
        private static string _eventCode = "GLS_21";
        private static DateTime _eventDate = new DateTime(2021, 06, 23);
        private static decimal[] _prices = new [] {
            100.50m, 260.65m, 540.10m
        };

        public ExternalTicketBookingController()
        {
        }

        [HttpGet]
        public IEnumerable<TicketInformation> GetTickets()
        {
            var tickets = new List<TicketInformation>();

            for (int i = 0; i < _prices.Length; i++)
            {
                tickets.Add(new TicketInformation()
                {
                    EventCode = _eventCode,
                    EventDate = _eventDate,
                    Price = _prices[_random.Next(_prices.Length)],
                    SeatCode = "NA",
                    Quantity = _capacity / _prices.Length
                });
            }

            return tickets;
        }
```

```csharp
[HttpPost("{seatCode?}")]
public async Task<IActionResult> ReserveTicket(string seatCode)
{
    await Task.Delay(1000);

    if (_random.Next(10) == 1)
    {
        return BadRequest();
    }
    return Ok();
}

[HttpPost("{seatCode?}")]
public async Task<IActionResult> PurchaseTicket(string seatCode)
{
    await Task.Delay(2000);

    if (_random.Next(10) == 1)
    {
        return BadRequest();
    }
    return Ok();
}
    }
}
```

We essentially have three possibilities here: we can retrieve the available tickets (since this example is not a seated event, the tickets are returned grouped by price), we can reserve a ticket (providing an optional seat code), or we can purchase a ticket (again, with an optional seat code).

The reserve and purchase methods have delay and potential failure built in so that we can simulate some of the real-world conditions of a real third-party API.

Note   The random number generator in .Net uses the time of day to generate the seed, which means that if you instantiate the Random class repeatedly in very quick succession and ask for a random number each time, you're likely to get the same number.

The takeaway from this is that we now have three endpoints. If you're following along, you should see where this API is listening (Figure A-1).

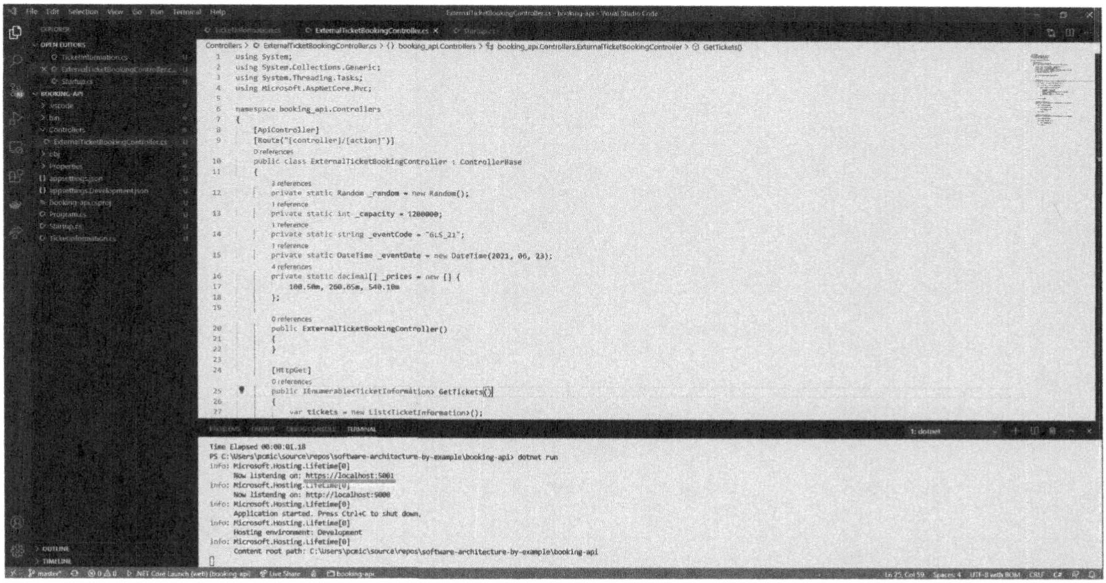

Figure A-1. *API output*

In my case (and likely in yours unless you explicitly change it), I'm listening on **https://localhost:5001**. The way that we've configured the routing, the endpoints will be as follows:

```
https://localhost:5001/externalticketbooking/gettickets
https://localhost:5001/externalticketbooking/reserveticket
https://localhost:5001/externalticketbooking/purchaseticket
```

Index

A

Admin Application problem
  examples
    CRUD function, 149, 151–154
    custom functionality, 156, 157
    extensibility, 154–156
  manual process, 127–129
  MVP, 126
  software
    hooks, 141, 142
    injection, 145–147
    messages, 142–144
  target architecture, 148
Ambassador Pattern, 162–166, 196
API output, 203
Architectural Decision Records (ADR), 91

B

Bulletin Board System (BBS), 93

C

CallCentralSystemCheckinFireAndForget
    method, 179
CallCentralSystemCheckin method, 179
CallCheckin method, 179
Cash desk
  CQRS, 46, 47
  event sourcing, 40–42
    aggregates, 46
    change immutable events, 43, 44

    immutable events, 42, 43
    projections/snapshots, 44, 45
  manual process, 33–36
  options, 32, 33
  persisting events to disk, 52
    load, 55, 57–60
    save, 53–55
    writing to files, 60, 61
  persisting events to
    memory, 49–51
  target architecture
    audit, 36–39
    diagram, 47, 48
ChaosMonkey function, 171
Command Query Responsibility
    Segregation (CQRS), 97
  benefits, 97–99
  consistency models, 100–102
  drawbacks, 99
CreateComment method, 117
CreatePost method, 117
CreateSinglePost method, 115
Customer Relationship Management
    (CRM), 126

D

Dependency Injection, 140, 141
Dependency Inversion Principle
    (DIP), 139
Distributed transaction, 63, 71, 74, 77,
    79, 90, 101

E, F, G, H

Eventual consistency model, 102
EZ Bolts, 32

I

Interface Segregation Principle, 137, 138
Inversion of Control (IoC), 140

J, K

JavaScript injection, 146

L

Liskov Substitution Principle (LSP), 135, 136
Lunar Polly Travel, 64, 160

M, N

Minimum viable product (MVP), 32, 126
Mock API, 200
MongoDB, 52, 104–107, 110, 111, 119

O

Open-Closed Principle, 129, 133, 157

P, Q

Proxy Pattern, 18, 164

R

ReadPosts method, 119–121

S

Send method, 134
Sidecar Pattern, 163–166
Social media

BBS, 93
CQRS, 122
definition, 93
example
checking data, 107
client application, 114–117
database, updating, 105, 106
MongoDB, 110–113
ProcessDataservice, 118–121
schema creation, 104
web service, 108, 109
requirements
CQRS, 97
manual process, 96, 97
options, 95
software, 94
target architecture, 102, 103
SOLID
definition, 129
DIP, 139, 140
interface segregation principle, 138
LSP, 136, 137
Open-Closed principle, 133–135
single responsibility principle
code churn, 131
definition, 130
software class, 132
software resilience, 132
testability, 131
SQL Server Management Studio
(SSMS), 107
System usage graph, 2

T, U, V

Target architecture, 8
choices, 10
cloud vendors, 19

diagram, 17

distributed service, 79

distributed transaction, 77

external APIs, 21

getting ticket availability, 21–24

logical flow, 78

message brokers, 14, 15

message queues, 13, 14

multiple funnels, 11, 12

ordering a ticket, 25

    Correlation ID, 27, 28

    message to queue, 25

    response to queue, 26

principle, 79, 80

private cloud, 20

proxy, 18, 19

proxy pattern, 18

separation of concerns, 16

stateful service, 79

widening the funnel, 10

    server, 10

    service, 10, 11

Ticket ordering system, 3

existing system, 6, 7

existing system considerations, 7

manual process, 4–6

minimum viable product, 8

options, 4

Travel agents

advanced purchase, 76

airport, 63

book/cancel, 75

business decision, 76

definition, 63

distributed transactions, 73, 74

distributed transactions,
    timeout, 74, 75

examples

coordinator, 85–90

    project structure, 80, 81

    service bus configuration, 82, 85

hold booking, 76

investigate system, 64

Lunar Polly Travel, 64

requirements

    high-level, 65

    manual process, 66, 67

    software design, 65

target architecture, 77

transactions

    account, 67, 90

    ACID, 67–70

    distributed transactions, 71–73

Travel Rep Problem

application, 160

central API, 170–172

containers

    displaying UI, 184

    Docker compose, 182, 183

durability, 195

functional requirements

    Ambassador pattern, 164–166

    caching, 162

    manual process, 161, 162

    sidecar pattern, 163

host machine, 184, 186, 187, 189,
    190, 192–195

project structure, 169

target architecture, 166–168

TravelRep.Ambassador, 174–181

TravelRep.App, 173, 174

W, X, Y, Z

Weather Forecast API, 200

Wrapper/proxy, 110

Printed in the United States
by Baker & Taylor Publisher Services